T0247445

Contemporary Theatre in Egypt

Edited by

Marvin Carlson

Martin E. Segal Theatre Center Publications

Frank Hentschker, Executive Director
Rebecca Sheahan, Managing Director

Martin E. Segal Theatre Center Publications
New York © 2016

Library of Congress Cataloging-in-Publication Data

Names: Symposium on Contemporary Egyptian Theatre (1999 : City University of
   New York) | Carlson, Marvin, 1935- editor.
Title: Contemporary theatre in Egypt / edited by Marvin Carlson.
Description: New York : Martin E. Segal Theatre Center Publications, 2016. |
   Proceedings of the Symposium on Contemporary Egyptian Theatre, held in
   February, 1999, at the City University of New York. | Includes
   bibliographical references.
Identifiers: LCCN 2016000468 | ISBN 9780990684787 (pbk.)
Subjects: LCSH: Theater--Egypt--History--20th century--Congresses. | Arabic
   drama--Egypt--History and criticism--Congresses. | Arabic drama--20th
   century--History and criticism--Congresses.
Classification: LCC PN2974 .S96 2016 | DDC 792.0962/0904--dc23 LC record
available at https://urldefense.proofpoint.com/v2/url?u=http-3A__lccn.loc.
gov_2016000468&d=CwIFAg&c=8v77JlHZOYsReeOxyYXDU39VUUzHxyfBUh7fw_
ZfBDA&r=r51pc3LFxbZcR3qtPw6WmF7RDa6sXfkKHkowJh6CVIo&m=cixbZnq_fBa9aqako5aHlDpTjBcQ9jhwz-
6kEE2A8ZU&s=c5gTNO-wi-KrCgHhIyYVoKkIhx-GlQZNZ9ik7XR6iYg&e=

Content Editor (Second Edition)
Yu Chien Liu

Cover Design (Second Edition)
Michael LoCicero

Second Edition

©2016 Martin E. Segal Theatre Center

Contemporary Theatre in Egypt

Edited by

Marvin Carlson

The Last Walk

The Absent One

The Nightmare

Acknowledgements

The February 1999 Symposium on Contemporary Egyptian Theatre and the accompanying performances were made possible by the financial and organizational support of the Egyptian Supreme Council of Culture and particularly its Secretary General, Dr. Gaber Asfour, by the Theatre Committee organ of the council, chaired by Alfred Farag, and by the Sidney E. Cohn and Lucille Lortel Chairs of Theatre Studies at the Graduate School and University Center of the City University of New York. Dr. Wagdi Zeid, currently Egyptian Cultural Attaché in Washington, was instrumental in organizing the event, as was Dalia Basinony, an Egyptian student in the Graduate Center Ph.D. program. Important contributions were also made by other students in the program both in organizing and running the symposium and in performing *The Person*.

The appearance of this publication is one of an ongoing series of events and publications devoted to Egyptian-American cultural relationships and co-sponsored by the Egyptian government and the City University of New York. This publication will be officially presented at an event at the Egyptian Cultural and Educational Bureau in Washington sponsored by the Egyptian Minister of Higher Education, Professor Mufeed Sheban and the Egyptian Cultural and Educational Councilor, Dr. Osama Zaki.

The publication of these proceedings and accompanying material has been made possible by support from the Sidney E. Cohn and Lucille Lortel Chairs.

Table of Contents

Proceedings of the Symposium
1. Greetings and Opening Remarks

FRANCES DEGAN HOROWITZ: It is really my pleasure to welcome you here to the Graduate School and University Center. Some of you may know that the Graduate School and University Center is that part of the City University of New York responsible for doctoral level programs and we organize doctoral education on a consortial model whereby we draw upon the faculty from all of the campuses of the City University of New York as well as the faculty located here to provide very high quality doctoral education. We have thirty-two doctoral programs with almost four thousand students and our doctoral programs are recognized all over this country and internationally as being of excellent quality. Among these of course is the theatre program. This is an especially wonderful evening and I regret that after a short word I am going to have to go on to another commitment, because I really would have liked to have stayed and have heard these plays. It is very nice and an honor to have these leading playwrights including Dr. Farag with us, and I would also like to thank Dr. Zeid, our alum, whom we proudly claim, for his help and also for his presence. I had a brief but wonderful several days that I spent in Egypt, where I feasted on *halawah* and met with colleagues, some of the eminent psychologists in Cairo and was taken out to surrounding villages where I visited one of the village schools and watched the education in progress and I hope that someday I will have the opportunity to go back for a longer stay. We are very pleased. This may be a first in New York, perhaps a first in the United States and one of the last here because in June the University Center will pack up and move to a new location a few blocks from here at

5

34ᵗʰ Street and Fifth Avenue. For those of you who are old New Yorkers, you may think of that as the old B. Altman Department Store, but most importantly, we are going to have expanded facilities for various kinds of public programs, including a small black box theatre where we hope there will be opportunities for playreadings and for new, young playwrights. I am sure you are in for a delightful evening and I envy you the opportunity to see these plays. Welcome.

WAGDI ZEID: On page 16 of the new *Larousse Encyclopedia of Mythology* we read the following: "Osiris wished to spread the benefits of his word throughout the whole world. Osiris was the enemy of all violence It was by gentleness alone that he could disarmed the inhabitants, and the playing of musical instruments. He returned to Egypt only after he had traveled over the whole world and spread civilization everywhere." This is knowledge. In real life, and thousands of years later, the Egyptian President Anwar Sadat went to Jerusalem for a peace that put an end to long years of war, destruction, and suffering. Under the leadership of Hosni Mubarek Egypt has managed not only to rebuild itself from inside but to establish relations of peace, mutual understanding and respect with the world's nations. This conference, held by CUNY, on Egyptian drama and the teaching or Egyptian and Arabic drama to American students are giant steps in the process of mutual understanding between the peoples of America and Egypt. The performance of two recent Egyptian plays and the participation of American and Egyptian scholars and the American presentation of the new anthology of English translations of recent Egyptian plays. This is indeed a very important cultural event in American-Egyptian relations.. On behalf of the Egyptian playwrights, scholars and artists. On behalf

6

of the General Secretary of the Supreme Council of Culture, Professor Gabor Asfour, and on behalf of the Minister of Culture of Egypt, Mr. Farouk Hosni, and myself, I would like to express deep gratitude to Distinguished Professor Carlson, and all CUNY members who made this great event possible. Thank you Professor Carlson. Thank you Madame President of CUNY. Thank you all CUNY members, and thank you America [applause].

MARVIN CARLSON: And now just a word of two of welcome, in another role, as a member of the theatre program. As Professor Horowitz has remarked to you, we're very proud of the theatre program here at CUNY. It is one of the most distinguished theatre programs in the country. It has long been a program that, while it is very much concerned with the American theatre and American theatre activity, it is also a program that has from the very beginning been extremely interested in and conscious of traditions in other countries and in other cultures.. Arabic drama is a new interest for us and I hope it will be a continuing and strong one, and we're very pleased to be able to do this. I extend particular thanks at this point in the program to the two endowed chairs that have been largely responsible for the funding of this program. The Sidney E. Cohn Chair, which I hold, and the Lucille Lortel Chair, which is held by Distinguished Professor Daniel Gerould. The next part of the program will be the presentation of two plays by Alfred Farag, who is speaking to us later, as well. The first play runs about forty minutes. The second play runs about eight or nine minutes, and for that play, since it is a short play, we have decided to give it twice, first in Arabic and then in English. So I'll turn the program now over to our actors.

2. Presentation of Two Plays by Alfred Farag

The Person, translated by Dina Amin
Performers

Hillary Arlen	Sharon Green
Henry Hamilton	Patricia Herrera
Lars Myers	Dierdre O'Leary
Handan Ozbilgin	Jennifer Starbuck
Marion Wilson	

Designed by Melissa Gaspar
Directed by Dalia Basiouny

The Last Walk, translated by Dina Amin
The Woman   Vanya Exerjian

Directed by Dina Amin

3. Roundtable Discussion on Contemporary Egyptian Theatre

The Panelists

Dina Amin has an MFA in directing from Carnegie Mellon University and is currently a Ph.D. candidate at the University of Pennsylvania, writing her dissertation on Alfred Farag's drama. She directed the premiere of *The Last Walk* in Cairo last summer.

Dalia Basiouny is a theatre practitioner and academic. She teaches drama in Helwan University, Cairo and has directed 11 plays. She has a B.A. from Cairo University, an M.A. from Bristol University, and is now in New York on a Fulbright Fellowship.

Vanya Exerjian is a graduate of the American University in Cairo where she majored in Psychology and Theatre. She is a permanent member of the Egyptian theatre troupe, al-Warshah, and has premiered many of its main roles. She created the room of the Woman in *The Last Walk* last summer in Cairo.

Atef El-Ghamri is President and Bureau Chief of the leading Egyptian newspaper *Al-Ahram.*. He is also a playwright, whose best known drama is probably *The Man at the Top* (1990).

Lenin El-Ramly, leading Egyptian playwright, born 1945, has successfully written for T.V. and cinema, as well as the theatre. 28 of his plays have been produced in most of the country's theatres. Probably his best known play internationally is *In Plain Arabic* (1991).

Alfred Farag, leading Egyptian playwright, born 1929. He

9

was granted the gold medal from the Supreme Council of Arts and Literature for his first one-act play, *Egypt's Voice*. He received the National Award for Playwriting in 1965 and the Science and Arts Medal in 1967. Among his many plays, probably the best known internationally is *The Caravan* (1968).

Gamal Abdel Maqsoud, leading Egyptian playwright, born 1942, is currently finishing his Ph.D. in the Department of English in Cairo University. He began his literary career as a short story writer, publishing his first one-act play in 1967. Probably his best known play internationally is *The Man Who Ate a Goose* (1990).

Wagdi Zeid, Appointed Egyptian Cultural Attache in Washington in 1999, received his Ph.D. in Theatre from the Graduate Center of the City University of New York. He is also a playwright, whose *Winter Dreams* was produced at the Graduate Center in 1988.

CARLSON: Actually, I was so stirred by the play we have just seen that it's difficult to settle down and have a calm discussion. It was really quite wonderful. I want to just make a very brief introduction. I could spend the next half hour talking about the qualifications of our distinguished panel, and later on I am going to ask a number of them to give a brief statement about their work and their feelings about the contemporary Egyptian theatre. Just now I call you attention to the fact that there are very very brief biographical statements in this evening's program. Let me then quickly introduce the panel starting from my far right. Our first two participants are this evening's two directors, Dina Amin and Dalia Basouany. Dina is a triple, or quadruple threat, not only being a wonderful director as you have seen, but also a critic and the translator of the two productions that we saw this evening [applause]. Next is Lenin El-Ramly, a playwright whose play, *In Plain Arabic* gave great delight to my Arabic theatre course this year. Next, Alfred Farag, who wrote both of the plays that we saw this evening [applause]. To my left my good friend Wagdi Zeid, whom I have already introduced once this evening. Then Gamal Maqsoud, the distinguished playwright. He also gave us great pleasure in my class this year with his *The Man Who Ate a Goose*. Then Atef Al-Ghamri, also a playwright and also the Bureau Chief and President of *Al-Ahram* newspaper, and finally, of course, Vanya Exerjian, our wonderful actress this evening [applause].

What I propose to do in this necessarily brief session is to begin with questions to the people who were involved with the productions, to make some comments about that work, then I will turn to the other panelists and ask them each to give a bit of introduction to themselves and their work and then, if time permits, we will have a more general discussion among ourselves about the current Egyptian theatre, but if time is pressing we will go right on the last part, since I do want to leave some time for members of the audience to ask questions about the productions tonight or to ask questions of any member of our distinguished panel. I also want to leave time for the reception afterward and for everyone to have a chance to converse and meet each other. Around 10:15 or 10:30 the security people come through and start closing the building down {laughter] so I will be always watching my watch.

I would first of all like to ask a question to Vanya which interests me very much. Both of the versions were powerful and fascinating, but I wonder, from an actress's point of view, in playing this piece in Arabic and in English, were there certain aspects that were in your opinion more powerful or more interesting in one language than in the other?

EXERJIAN: Well, I would say that the first time I read this play with Dina in English I remember she told me "This sounds like a woman in a Shakespearian play; she sounds like Lady Macbeth or something, " so it was very interesting in working together with Dina we used the same tools that an Egyptian story-teller, an Egyptian woman who was telling this story, would use in order to do this play. We used Egyptian story-telling tools. Otherwise it would be very very different. I you started with "Once upon a time..." it would be very different. But I must also say that Dina has done a very good job translating it because the first Arabic version of course with Mr. Farag, I enjoyed playing it because it was written for an actor. It was very easy for an actor to do it. And Dina's translation I think was very good as well and succeeded in helping me do that.

12

CARLSON: Did the translation change as you worked on it, as the dynamics of acting took over?

AMIN: As a translator you want to be literal, but when you get on stage you want to be closer to the spoken language, so eventually we made some changes, with Mr. Farag's permission of course, because he is responsible for his work and his words to you are not allowed to change anything as you work [laughs]. But of course there were a number of considerations in doing it in English after the Arabic The rural Egyptian colloquial that was used in the Arabic must maintain the rhythm. Some of you may think that was the actress; of course, she does have an accent, but the way she sort of meandered in her speech was to render this colloquial language pattern.

CARLSON: Just watching the production, I was able to see very little difference in the physical movement, the gestures, and so on. Were you aware of distinct changes you had to make in order to fit a different language?

EXERJIAN: No, actually, Dina asked me to keep everything the way it was. Otherwise it would have been a completely different production

AMIN: It sounded as if we did not do that. It sounded very stiff.

CARLSON: This is not so much a question about the production as a question about the Egyptian theatre. This form has become much more popular in the American theatre in recent years, that is, the one-person production, and I wondered how common it is in the current Egyptian theatre.

AMIN: Well, Mr. Farag did monodramas in the 1960s and continues to do so, so perhaps he would like to comment on this.

CARLSON: Mr. Farag?

FARAG: It's a form that's easy, easy to do at schools, at clubs, the one-person show, the one-person performance. I like to give it to the young people who are practicing acting. Of course *The Person* is a play for one person, but Dalia did it with ten persons [laughter]. That doesn't mean I don't like it, I like it very much, but I wonder, and I want to ask her that question. Is it because she wants more people to participate. That's an idea, there is a philosophy.

BASIOUNY: I had the impression that the person is more than one person, that he is everyone, he is young and old, mature and immature...

FARAG: Thank you, that's enough [laughter].

CARLSON: I have a question for Dalia that is something of a variation of a question that I asked of Vanya and Dina and again it is trying to get a feel, particularly from those of you who have been fortunate enough to have been involved in theatre work both in Egypt and in the United States, of the differences. Dalia, you've done a reasonable amount of directing in Egypt and I realize that this was a very brief amount of work with American students. I guess first of all I should ask you, have you ever directed English-speaking actors before?

BASIOUNY: Yes, I did in England.

CARLSON: So these are your first Americans?

BASIOUNY: Yes.

CARLSON: Well, then that makes my question a bit more complicated, I guess. Given the fact that you have not been doing this for six months, but only for two weeks. I'm curious if you have any observations about the differences in working with actors in Egypt, and if you like in England, and in the United States? American actor training is rather different from English, and, I imagine, from Egyptian. Did you notice differences in working with the actors?

BASIOUNY: I can't agree more with that. I is very different in acting styles and methods. The challenge of this play was to give an Egyptian feel with American actors. So I tried to explain a little bit about the situation from an Egyptian point of view but this was not easy to maintain in the whole process, so I thought that the actors would do an American version of the play. Most of the actors I believe are trained in realistic or naturalistic acting. In England it is more expressionistic acting, if I may call it that.

CARLSON: From time to time I would see a movement or a gesture and I would think "That's very American." but not in an unpleasant or negative way. Indeed at one point—I don't know whether this is in the original text or not—the physical mirror scene is very interesting and that is also a very well-known American acting exercise.

BASIOUNY: We have it in Egypt also [laughter]

CARLSON: That's interesting to know.

15

BASIOUNY: That was part of the text. There was one person and one double, and we were more generous.

CARLSON: OK. Unless some member of the panel would like to ask some question about the particular productions, I'd like to move on to the panel itself. Would either of the directors like to say anything before we move on?

BASIOUNY: I would just like to say that this is not the whole of the play. Because of time limits we could not do the whole.

CARLSON: We got a sample of each scene of the play.

BASIOUNY: Yes.

CARLSON: About how long would the play run?

BASIOUNY: We did a little bit more than half, so probably about an hour and ten minutes.

ZEID: I would like to say that what fascinates me in the two plays is Farag's treatment of the self and the other and how the self is dominated by the other. We are concerned all the time with the self and how it discovers itself in terms of the other and of the self itself. What I like about the production by Dalia and her friends is that she analyzed, signified, this relationship between the self and the other. Remember the doubles scenes, the one and the other, the one and the other. I liked this very much.

CARLSON: I don't know if I mentioned this before and I really must. All of the students in this production are students in our graduate program and I think that all of them, or almost all of them were students in the Arabic theatre class. This is a way that they have been able to move on to a more embodied sense of what they were studying last term which of course is a wonderful educational tool also.

Now I'd like to move on and ask each one of our playwright guests to say something about their career, whatever they might like to say about it, and also, if they could, to say something about the contemporary theatre scene in Egypt, the contemporary state of theatre. I think it is most proper to start with Dr. Farag.

FARAG: As for my career, it started in the 1950s. I had some plays that were hits and others that were less than hits. I write normally in very different, I can't say styles, but different atmospheres. I write some plays in colloquial Arabic and some plays in classical Arabic. It depends on the subject. I write comedies, I write tragedies, I have written also one drama and social dramas. I don't like to repeat myself and to stay in one place. I like to go from here to there. Of course this play, *The Person*, is a philosophical play. It is not a repeat of anything I have done before. My audience likes me, I wish censorship could be more tolerant or as tolerant as my audience. Because of course, good theatre is an attack on the audience. People like theatre to change society, that is, they are not happy with this society. They want to change or they want the people who are listening to change, so theatre is an attack on the auditorium. But I am happy to say that I have been applauded and cheered for that by the audience, but not by everyone else maybe [laughter].

Of course the Egyptian theatre traditionally has a long history, starting back in the mid-nineteenth century, but the folkloric theatre goes back to the middle ages, maybe before. Some archeologists also tell us about a ritual play of very ancient times. But I am not satisfied with the scene of Egyptian theatre. I think that Egyptian theatre could do better, and could be more spread through the country, because it is concentrated in Cairo and everywhere else it is more amateur theatre. The professional theatre is always in Cairo, which I don't like. I hope that theatre in Egypt will do better. I think also that Egyptians love theatre. One German director told me when he visited Egypt "The best thing in your theatre is the audience. Because they are very warm. We have a very warm audience, an audience that gives the artist the prize in response. They are very lively. When you want to make them laugh they laugh. They are impressed very deeply and they show it to the artist. So it is an atmosphere of great magic in our theatre because of the excellent audience. I think that is all. [applause]

CARLSON: I think I will move to my right and then to my left, so Doctor El-Ramly?

EL-RAMLY [in Arabic]: I started writing in the mid seventies. I wrote for the so called private sector theatre [commercial theatre]. I wrote about twenty-nine plays, and I produced too. After a while I preferred to have my own company to produce the kind of plays I wanted to do.

I am proud of myself because I reached the audience directly without the support or interference of the state. In spite of that, I was able to present —through the private sector— experimental plays. I did experiments with young amateurs. I believe this was an important issue for me, to present experiments with the young actors, one of which is a play that, I believe, had a big impact and a lot was written about it in America, in many of the American newspapers,

18

that's *In Plain Arabic.*

I also wrote different kinds of plays, most of them in a comic frame, as they say. In spite of the fact that they don't have happy endings. Some people think I wrote political plays, I believe I write about the patterns of thinking, our way of rationalizing. As expected, these plays caused various reactions, some people liked them, others didn't. I believe it's important that one should capture the audience whether or not one agrees or disagrees with the audience or pleases them [applause].

CARLSON: Moving to my left now, another distinguished Egyptian dramatist Gamal Maqsoud

MAQSOUD: I would like to add a few words on tonight's performance, then move on to my statement. What we saw tonight, Mr. Farag's one-act plays show him as a challenger. Mr. Farag swims against the tide, as far as theatre is concerned. For example, repetition has a bad reputation and all playwrights, especially in playwrights on playwriting advise new playwrights to avoid repeition on the grounds that it is boring. But Mr. Farag puts repetition to a good use. The repetition of the complaints is not boring. It gives us a laugh. It was functional. This reminds one of what Brecht says, The proof of the pudding is in the eating. And Mr. Farag's new use of repetition is quite competent, efficient and functional. Besides, Mr. Farag uses two other devices pertaining to other genres, narration and poetic language. As far as poetic language is concerned the theme says keep away from poetic language, keep to everyday language. Martin Esslin has a different point of view. He opts for poetic language on special instances. Mr. Farag sides with Martin Esslin and he takes his point of view to some

19

extremes and is successful. Narration belongs to the novel and Mr. Farag uses it in the two one-act plays, the Last Walk and the Person yet he uses words sparingly and he uses this device, which is considered alien to the theatre very efficiently. We have a playwright who has his own individual independent full-fledged work and I say praise him for this contribution {applause}

Now to move on to myself. It is difficult to speak of oneself, yet I will add a few words. I started writing plays in 1967. I wrote a tragedy [*The Absent One*, published in this volume–ed.]. Now I am known for writing comedies and this play, *The Man Who Ate a Goose*, is a comedy but I started with a lucky tragedy. It was in one act and it was lucky because it was in the theatre not in Egypt but in French academic circles. It was the topic of two famous books on the theatre, *Le theatre arabe* and *L'Histoire du romanesque d'Egypt moderne*. Written by the Sorbonne professor Dr. Madat Thoms. A playwright to me has two functions and he has to perform these in a certain way. He has to carry a message, and he has to deliver it in an amusing way to attract an audience, because I agree with my colleague that the audiences are a very important side of the theatrical performance. So what is serious in one's writing is the message and the medium is the comic devices. I end my report on myself with a paragraph from a study of my play by a a famous Egyptian critic. "He is another master of modern drama in Egypt, picked as his basic theme the fate of modern man and his helplessness between the grinding stones of capitalism and fake brands of socialism. He also tapped the popular conv ventions of dramatic art and humor and the public response to the words of this physician turned playwright was remarkably lively. Gamal Abdel Maqsoud shifted the emphasis from abstract notions and conceptional groundwork toward more concretized treatment of private cases which developed to take on phenomenal proportions. His main contribution has been the attempt to create in a refined manner a balance between the needs of the fun-seeking theatre-goer and constraits of the sober text writer who writes with a theme in mind. Maqsoud's comedies, which are mostly based on aspects of daily human existence, neither have the simplistic happy ending of the commercial theatre nor the tired didactic ending of the more earnest comedies in current circulation. Moreover, his idea of realism is essentially crystallized around a private case which is not occurring mechanically rather it is put to the test in a variety of a situations ultimately reaching its rational conclusion which paradoxically smacks of fantasy. However it is a crucial kind of fantasy from which the audience infers the importance of having a sense of rational self-defense rather than waiting in the sun for the just despot who will rid them of their social ills and political oppression." Thank you. [applause]

CARLSON: To Dr. Maqsoud's left is Dr. Atef Al-Ghamri. As I mentioned earlier, Dr. Al-Ghamri, who is himself a playwright but who is perhaps as well known or better known to you as the president and bureau chief of *Al-Ahram*, a very distinguished international newspaper and in my opinion has the best reportage of any of the Arabic newspapers about cultural events in Egypt in general and on the theatre in particular. If Dr. Al-Ghamri wishes to say something from his position as playwright that would be fine but I would also be curious, given his key position on the cultural scene as a cultural commentator if he would have anything to say generally on his observations about the current theatre scene in Egypt.

AL-GHAMRY: Of course all my colleagues are older than me, I am the youngest [laughter]. I began my first play in 1983, it was performed by the national theatre, and from that day on, as I mention the titles of my plays, I can notice that all of them or most of them have focused on one theme, the metaphor of expression and freedom. The first play, *The Man at the Top* and there was also a drama.[brief discussion in Arabic among Al-Ghamri, Maqsoud, and Zeid concerning play titles}

ZEID: How fascinating our Arabic language is. It can hide a lot as well.

AL-GHAMRY: Maybe because I am a journalist I write on politics and that is why I noted that it is not intentional, but finally after I finish I find that I am still dealing with political subjects. I think that's all [applause]

CARLSON: I notice that almost every one of our playwright panelists has remarked on how important confrontation with the audience is, and so clearly it is time to move on and given them a chance to confront you [laughter]. At this time I would be delighted to entertain questions from the audience to anyone on the panel or general questions to which anyone on the panel can respond if they wish. We have mikes on both sides. If you can handily get to one, please do so. Yes, in the back.

QUESTION: Do any of your plays reflect any specific events that are going on in Egypt in recent times?

MAQSOUD: Art is different from journalism. It is not necessary that art keep close to everyday events. It takes some time for ideas to be mature and ferment in the minds. The theatre differs a bit from the press. This is the function of the press, to follow everyday events. But art or the theatre in general has to keep in mind all the old lines, not only the detailed events. So the reply is for the time being there are no plays that reflect what is taking place on the scene of events in Egypt.

CARLSON: We have another one or two of the panelists who have a slightly different view. Let's hear.

AMIN: Well I hope you don't mind my commenting. Who does not take the bus to go to the doctor or take the train to upper Egypt. There cannot be more everyday activities than in *The Person*. Secondly *The Last Walk*, I am only talking about the plays that we saw today, of course we can apply the same criteria to plays that are written by Drs. Maqsoud or El-Ramly. *The Last Walk*, as you probably have felt is the dilemma of a woman, not only in Egypt but all over the world. So I do think that Egyptian drama does reflect everyday life and deals with contemporary problems.

EL-GHAMRY: If I understand your question, about how drama deals with current events. My last play in Egypt in 1993 was involved with terrorism. Terrorism is not a local phenomenon, but involves the whole world, as you know. That means that we in drama write on any subject. We are not isolated from events locally or internationally.

QUESTION: I agree very much with the idea that theatre should address itself to changing reality, I would like you to address the question of censorship. How do you work with this? In communist countries theatre people usually found a way to get around this by trying to convey messages through clever adaptations of classics and their audiences got their messages. How far can

23

you go without getting into trouble. That's what I would like to ask.

MAQSOUD: Rest assured that as far as censorship is concerned, in Egypt now there is complete freedom now. In the past we used to resort to strategies to get around censorship. But now we say whatever we please. This is an honest and frank system. In this respect there is complete freedom now.

AMIN: It seems I am the right wing here and I must say I completely disagree with this statement [applause] and perhaps Mr. Farag can comment..

CARLSON: Dina has challenged Dr. Farag to comment on this.

FARAG: Well, frank censorship no longer exists in Egypt, but we have some seven veils of censorship [laughter]. When you are a play author and courageous you don't go on television, the play doesn't go on television and if you ask they say your play is very boring, and if you are less bold, perhaps the play doesn't run long enough on stage. Some plays don't have the facilities to go abroad, and so on. Of course, we don't feel perfectly all right, but then the situation is better than it was before and we hope it will be better in the future. Please note that I myself do not think that censorship is a proper thing in a modern democratic society, but we hope for better in the future [applause].

EL-RAMLY: I want to say that censorship in our country is not a problem now-a- days. I'd like to add that there is a difference between censorship in the theatre and cinema, and that in television, it's more severe in television. I want to add that there is another important element, that of the censorship of society itself. Society can practice censorship from within, not needing anyone from outside forcing society to do it [applause].

ZEID: I would like to add that censorship is a very tough question. Even in America here we have some productions that might be taken to be too much. For example, Karen Finley, yes she will be allowed to do things, but she will be fought against in many ways. There are degrees of censorship, how far we can go with what we can say. It is as problem, has been a problem and will remain a problem.

BASIOUNY: I disagree with most of the other panelists. I think that most of the artists in Egypt practice self-censorship in order not to get into trouble. I know that there are hundreds of plays that I would love to put on stage but I will not able to. Sometimes I try to push the limit a little bit more, but because I want to continue to work there I practice self-censorship and either cut those scenes or not do this play so it is a big influence there. Trying to put on the play and not have the money for it if it doesn't go with what is allowed at this point in time. Of course, things have improved dramatically recently but there is still a different kind of censorship, mainly financial. For me I cannot put on a play that this particular manager would not like or the people in power would not be in favor of. Thank you. [applause]

CARLSON: We are near the end of the time. I am going to take two more questions.

QUESTION: She said that some plays she cannot or might not present. You have to say what are the comments you are not allowed to make.

FARAG: What is the question?

CARLSON: The question is what sorts of topics in terms of self-censorship do you feel that you must be cautious about?

BASIOUNY: I am not that cautious. I have translated a play by a Timberlake Wertenbaker, who is an English/Canadian playwright, and it is about violence against women and I have tried for two years to raise money to do the play and haven't been successful. I have the full project ready if I find the stage and the money and they will never be there. It is about violence against women.

AMIN: As a matter of fact I have a very concrete example. I translated a play that was written by an upcoming playwright for the Eugene O'Neill Center Arab project and it was denied performance....

AUDIENCE MEMBER: Why?

AMIN: Because it was a story about two people who have been engaged for seven years and cannot get married.

AUDIENCE MEMBER: Everybody has to admit that Egypt takes care of writers   We have right now some kind of freedom in what we have...more than before... and I'm sure that Mr. Alfred Farag and Mr. El-Ramly and everybody here can say more now that what they could say some time ago. That's number one. Number two. Theatre is not like television. Even now, in America, this year, we have started to have censorship aimed at television, in America, OK? So can we have in Egypt open theatre? Our culture does not permit it. You cannot have that. You cannot have whatever you want in theatre.

CARLSON: A point that several people have made is that there

26

are many, many different   kinds of censorship, particularly in an art like the theatre, which is a public art. You can of course write a play privately, circulate it among your friends—all right, but that isn't theatre. It really isn't theatre until you go out and display it before a public. And one of the prices that we in the theatre pay for this in every country, in every culture is that the theatre is therefore more susceptible to a whole variety of pressures, more than the other arts. This has always been true. Of course here in the United States we have no, or not much of an official censorship but everybody who works in the theatre in the United States knows that there are all kinds of difficulties in writing...I mean you can write anything you want but can you get it produced, can you get some television station to pick it up? Of course not! There's all kinds of economic pressures, and there we go back to the public, and who's paying for it, and whatever. I do think that everyone in the theatre wants to and should struggle for the freest expression possible, but I think that we should recognize that it is a continual struggle and I think that no theatre culture that I am aware of is totally free of it. Now we are getting to the end of the hour. All right, here's what we're going to do. This person over at the microphone will speak, Wagdi will speak, Dalia will speak And then, I will speak [laughter] This is censorship.

AUDIENCE MEMBER: I just want to add something here. Mr. Lenin El-Ramly is one of the most interesting theatre writers in Egypt, and not only in Egypt, in the Arabic world. And in the last ten years he is one of the most interesting writers and he did many plays that will never be played, at least not in these times. *A Point of View* et cetera, et cetera, and about censorship. Right now there is no censorship of the sort that you have in mind. But our society is absolutely different from American society. You can't compare censorhip in our society and censorship in American society. If you are going to compare American and Egyptian censorship in theatre then you have to compare American and Egyptian society in all aspects, in everything. You can't compare Egyptian society with American society when it comes to theatre. And right now we have sixty or seventy-five percent of freedom, which is great.

ZEID: Those Egyptians here, if you don't remember, Sami [the last speaker] was an actor himself. Do you remember him? [applause]

BASIOUNY: Some of the panelists and people in the audience insinuated that the Egyptian psyche is underage and needs protection. I do not accept this notion. Egyptian society is a society that can accept any play. I mean, who is to decide when this society is grown up and can take this play? [applause]

CARLSON: I am going to back off a little. Dr. Farag has asked me for half a minute, which I will give him, and Dr. El-Ramly, who has been spoken of, should have a chance to say something. So I'll ask Dr. El-Ramly to speak first and then Dr. Farag.

EL-RAMLY: [In Arabic] I'd like to clarify what I have said about society's censorship. I am going to disagree with you [Dalia].. you said the society can accept anything.. I believe the reality of the situation is different, or else there would have been no problems. If we left the theatre, cinema and art would suffer. Of course our society has its problems. Of course there are people in our society who reject things and express this violently. [audience response.. to this he answers] It's not a matter of all societies. I am a writer and I believe I'd rather say all what I want, of course I will be a different person, but I believe, without any connection to censorship or the government. Now, at this point of time, there is a form of censorship even in what we are saying now, not from an outside force, but from ourselves. There are different currents in the society. You are talking about governmental censorship. The government says, for example, this actress shouldn't wear this costume on stage.. this is understood. But you can perform the same play in a different place or even on a different night and the audience themselves would prevent this.. This is what I call "society's censorship'.. you can't say this doesn't exist. There are limits. If the government allowed the actress to go naked on stage, I, as a playwright, director, or producer, can't do that even if the government allows it.

CARLSON: A brief statement now from Dr. Farag, and then I have an announcement to make.

FARAG: Unfortunately, somebody changed the subject of the evening. The fellow over there, instead of telling us whether or not he enjoyed the plays, he took us away from that to discuss censorship in Egypt. We do not have any objection to discussing anything in Egypt. We can discuss that in Egypt and abroad. We are not embarrassed to say that in Egypt, a developing country, we should do so and so, or we want complete freedom of the theatre or of television. It doesn't embarrass us to say so, because the Americans say so also, for television, for films, for everything. We are the intelligensia. We are the intelligent ones. We want to change the world. Not only Egypt or the Arab world. We want to change the world. We are trying to express our desire for a changed world, for a happier world.

29

Why should this embarrass anybody or upset anybody?
It doesn't upset us. We are the artists. We are those
who create things and who leap in the dark We may
step on a mine that explodes or land in a paradise or
land wrongly in the abyss. So give us the courage to
do whatever we like because art is all about
change—changing the minds and the hearts of the
people. We want to live in a happier world, and not
only oppose the Egyptian censorship but also oppose
the American censorship, which has drawn a line
before the Arabic countries and Arabic plays
{applause] We don't have any plays in the world
repertoire, or in the American repertoire. Why? They
have plays from Romania, from Bulgaria, even from
Asia, from India, China, and Japan. Why shouldn't
there be Egyptian, Arabic plays in the repertoire? So
we should criticize America here. Why should we
criticize the Egyptian censorship or whatever? We are
criticizing the world. We are the artists. It is our
profession to criticize the whole world [applause] and
I begin here tonight be criticizing America. And I am
not embarrassed by my country or by its censorship. I
have told you that I am not satisfied with the Egyptian
theatre scene. Don't be embarrassed to hear that,
because we want Egypt to be the best country, the top
country, the country of freedom and happiness and
everything. Why do we write? We don't write to be
paid for what we write. We write to make people
happier, to enjoy. We write for an audience that enjoys
everything and we enjoy them enjoying our plays. So
let's be happy [applause].

CARLSON: Once again, as after the production, I feel that
anything that I say will be anticlimactic, but that won't
stop me. Actually, the wonderful words from Dr.
Farag serve as a very nice transition into what I am in

fact supposed to do at this point. Certainly I couldn't agree more with the expression of concern and the wish and desire that indeed the Arabic theatre and the Egyptian theatre in particular be given more attention than the shameful neglect that they've had in American culture. A number of us are working on this, believe me, including several in the audience, and of course this evening's event, small as it is in the whole cultural context, is an important gesture in that way, and indeed I think that my experience, forgive me for speaking as an American and not at all as a member of the Egyptian cultural scene. My experience, often, in speaking with my Egyptian friends about the Egyptian theatre and Egyptian culture there is often a feeling of "Well, we have these problems and we have those problems and it would be so much better if we didn't have them." I think any artist has that side. But I think that whatever problems Egyptian playwrights have, now and in the recent past, my students I am sure, will witness that this has not resulted in mediocre or uninteresting plays. There are wonderful, wonderful plays out of Egypt and indeed those of you, and I imagine there are some in the audience, who have never seen an Egyptian play performed before can judge simply by what we saw this evening. There is a rich and wonderful acting tradition going on here whatever problems they may have with censorship or whatever else the dramatists are concerned about. That's why its so wonderful for me to hear Dr. Farag make so positive a statement. If we are not familiar, we as Americans, with these plays, this is no fault of the plays, it's our fault. Now, connected with that, not only do have the great pleasure of having the experience, all too rare in New York, of seeing some wonderful plays very intelligently done, but I also want to take this occasion to call your attention to a major new translation project of Egyptian plays into English. As you were coming in, a number of you may have noticed the books on the tables. I think most of them have been picked up now but by all means if there are still some out there and you want to pick up a copy, do so. This is a wonderful translation project that the Secretary General of the Supreme Cultural Council of Egypt, Gabor Asfour, himself a very distinguished literary critic and patron of culture, has sponsored and worked very hard and very fast to make available to us for this meeting—a whole new set of major translations by a large number of major Egyptian playwrights, some of them with us tonight and some not. They are beautiful little books, the bindings are beautiful, the covers are lovely, the paper is nice, and they're wonderful translations. If you would like to have copies and you are unable to get them this evening, the Supreme Council for Culture is giving them away for free. You have only to contact them. Would that American were enlightened enough to have one of our cultural institutions give away free plays, but you only to contact them and they will be happy to send these to you. If you didn't see them, I do have sample copies that I will have out in the lobby. We have a very nice buffet of middle eastern food. I urge you all to join us and take the occasion now to continue discussing or congratulating. I thank you all for coming.

The Egyptian Theatre Translation Project

The following new translations of contemporary Egyptian plays were prepared under the direction of Dr. Gabor Asfour, Secretary General of of the Egyptian Supreme Council of Cultureandd were presented at the February symposium.

The House of Al-Doughry
by Nomaan Ashour
translated by Dr. Mohammed Abdel Aty
revised by Wagdi Zeid

Revenge: A Quest of Pain
by Mohammed Salamoni
translated by Professor Fatma Mousa and
Mohammed Al Gindi

Bawabet Al Fetouh
by Mahmood Diab
translated by Professor Fatma Mousa and
Dr. Amal Mazzhar

Layla and the Madman
by Salah Abdel Sabour
translated by Mohammed Enani

A Point of View
by Lenin El-Ramly
translated by Yousef Al-Hefnawi
revised by Wagdi Zeid

Notes on the Following Translations

The Last Walk was written at the translator's request for a one-woman show. In Arabic, Farag's greatest success in composing this play is finding a voice, an idiom and a language for the oppressed. The English translation attempts to transfer the gestures and style of the state of oppression into English. Slight adjustments have been made to make the translation smoother and easier to understand. A few words of Arabic were left in the translation, as their meanings were clear.

The Absent One, although the most conventional of these plays in its dramatic scenes, is an innovative as any in its use of language. Written in 1968, it was one of the first modern serious dramas to use colloquial dialect, normally the domain of comedy. The stylistic differences are not strongly marked in translation, but the reader should note how occasions for colloquial speech are created by the frequent use of quoted colloquial speech and the simple dialogues of the children.

The Nightmare does not rely upon normal dramatic dialogue but works more musically, by the association of ideas and the repetition of key phrases, a number of them quotations from popular songs, familiar classics, and children's rhymes that will be instantly familiar to an Egyptian audience, but not to a reader from outside that culture. In the translation we have tried to find approximate English translations, drawing upon the same sort of folk and popular material from this culture.

The Last Walk

by Alfred Farag

translated by Dina Amin

The Last Walk

THE WOMAN is tied to a post by a rope around her wrist and waist.

THE WOMAN: The one who hit me and tied me up like this
is my husband, not a stranger. He's the father of my
children. It isn't your business, you with curious
eyes that deserve to be shot with a bullet. I don't
care if I get beaten up, so long as the one who beats
me is my father or my brother. They have the right
to beat me up if they wish to. You want to untie the
rope? Don't even try or by God's Grace I'll scream
at the top of my lungs and gather the people around
you . . . ! They love me: my husband, my father, and
my brother. They're my family, and my family loves
me; they beat me because they are scared for me.
They tied me up? Of course they did; so that I don't
harm myself . . . injure myself , , , hurt myself. And
what if my own son hit me, what is it to you? As you
know, my husband took his kids and ran away from
me. Of course he did, because of my own wrong
doing! And the rope, which my husband has tied
around my wrist and waist, no one will untie but him
. . .

I never learned arithmetic, neither addition . . . nor
subtraction . . . so yesterday I went to the grocer
(with whom we have a tab; we buy and he writes it
all down in chalk, on the wall of his store). I bought
on credit, my God increase your bounty: honey and
cheese and soap and halavah and pepper and
coriander and some oil and a handful of olives and a
handful of okra and a bunch of fresh herbs. And I
took only one apple, to have a taste of it and have my
husband taste it too. I didn't make the arithmetic.

37

When my husband went by the grocer's store and
saw our balance on the wall, he came into the house
yelling like a lunatic, and said "You've impoverished
me, may God put your father in the poorhouse! You
must be in love with that grocer!" So, in my fright,
the okra got burnt and the pot fell on the beaker of
honey, which spilled over the pepper and cumin.
And the herbs fell over the halavah and then into the
coriander, and the oil over the apple and I had some
salt, which also fell on top of them. And the head of
garlic fell out of the window into the street; the
bastards in the street snatched it from one another
until its cloves disappeared. What remained of it was
a white and green stem . . . My husband tied me up
like this and took his kids and ran away.

What's with you? Are you enjoying this or are you
gloating or what? Leave the rope alone! He forgot
to untie me. He took his kids and ran away and
forgot to untie my hands. You're going to untie me?
What business is it of yours? How will I drink?
How will I eat? If I deserve a sip of water to quench
my thirst, God will release me from my distress and
will send an angel from heaven to untie my hands
and give me a sip of water. And if no angle comes
down to rescue me and set my hands free, well then
that'll surely be justice and God's will. It'll be my
fault for having upset my husband until he ran away
from me with my kids. There, it's my fate and
destiny, and a lesson to be learnt . . . Indeed, those
whose parents never taught them, will learn from
their daily trials . . . and this is my destiny and path
of learning.

I am thirsty!

They told me I was born on a sizzling hot day. The
day I was born, they looked into my eyes and said,
"Praise God, she isn't blind!" And then they
smacked me hard to make me scream. When I
screamed, they said, "Praise God, she isn't dumb!"
Then they beat drums near my ears. When they saw
I got startled, pulled away and screamed with fear,
they said, "Praise God, she isn't deaf!" The day I
walked. they said, "Praise God, the girl isn't
crippled!" When I lived, they said "Praise God, she
didn't get the evil eye!" But, all my life I've heard
them suck their lips and ask one another, "Why then
doesn't she have luck?" They never found out that I
was a good-for-nothing until I went to the village
school. It was full of boys, and whatever the boys
added, I subtracted, and what they subtracted, I
added, and what they multiplied, I divided . . . Hell!
I don't understand such things as numbers and
divisions and shares! So the teacher's assistant
would beat me up, and the master would clobber me.
The boy sitting next to me would slug me. The one
sitting behind me would pull my hair, and anyone
with a stick would hit me with it and anybody with a
board would bang me with it. They'd keep doing
that until I'd forget my name. When they'd call on
me, I wouldn't answer. So they'd repeat the beating
routing again. May God save us from ignorance and
the ignorant.

They made me stay home from school . . . to mop,
wash the dirty clothes, prepare breakfast, cook lunch
and dinner, clean and pull and push, feed the birds,
milk the cow, walk it, groom and graze it too. I took
care of the young ane attended to the old, and in the
morning, while doing my chores around the house,
I'd overhear them saying, "Tragedy will be the share

of the ond who marries her!" In the afternoon, I'd
hear them say, "What a calamity it will be for the one
who falls for her!" At sunset, I'd hear them say,
"What a disaster if we were stuck with her a
spinster!" And at night, I'd hear them say,

"People's calamities are this and that,
 With her, our misfortune exceeds all that."

When the person I was to marry finally came, they all
kept ululating day and night. My father beamed, and
my siblings laughed. They even borrowed money in
order to give out sherbet to the neighbors. They said,
"Indeed, this is strange, yet, God provides for the
birds in the sky."

"Every Jack has his Jill."
"Love is blind and luck's eyes are closed."

My father stopped beating me up. My brother
stopped beating me up too. No one called me names.
They would look at me while coming and going in
the house with astonishment . . At that time, they
remembered that I had never come down with
smallpox; that got dysentery only twice, and
inflammation of the eye once and recovered from it.
When they recalled all of that, they said, "No one
could have possibly cast a bad eye on this girl nor
made her a victim of it because of her incompetence,
her unpleasant character and attitude."

When I got married, my husband became the one
responsible for me. Only *he* could beat me up and
had the right too. He was so tender he'd only slug
me with a belt that had no buckle, or slap me across
the face *after* taking off his silver ring, or kick me

about *after* taking off his shoes. But he hated me, poor darling, every time I gave birth to one more child, for the load piled up on his shoulders. I'd then pray saying, "O God, the kids will make him run away from me. And he will make me run away from my kids. And my kids will make me run away from my husband."

The place became too small for us; we slept on the bed and the kids under it. The ones awake would disturb those sleeping. We all started yelling at each other, each screaming within themselves and at the top of their lungs. The passersby would tell each other as they came and went, "It's nor your business, the man is disciplining his kids." The walls kept shrinking and patience ran out. The bedspread contracted, the table narrowed. Life itself became cramped, and it shrank, and I continued saying 'O God, relieve us already!"

Afterwards my husband—the apple of my eye—realized that I had brought him bad luck, for he'd work one day, become idle the next. So I took a 25-piaster note from his pocket and when to Umm 'Agwah, to have her burn some incense for me. I wanted her to lift the bad luck off my husband. The woman said, "Relief is after two points: two days, or two months, or two years!"

After two days I became anxious, but after two months I couldn't sleep a wink. I started getting screaming fits for no reason at all. My husband started tying me up with a rope so I wouldn't harm myself, hurt myself, and between times he would give me some water and ask, "Do you need anything?" My heart would pound and I'd answer,

The Absent One

*The stage is divided into two parts, the first cannot be
seen by the audience and the second is a hall in a
poor, middle-class household. At the end of the hall
is a half-open window. A women in her forties,
dressed in black, is looking out. An older woman,
her mother, sits on the floor, mending a shirt.*
*The time is approaching sunset on a winter
day. The wind is heard whistling outside.*

THE OLD WOMAN (*to THE WOMAN*): They have nothing
to occupy them but the cat. After I have cleaned the
house and kicked the cat out, whoever gets home
from school first comes in with the cat in his arms.
At night they sneak it into the house, play with it, and
feed it bread. They never pick up a pen or open a
book (*silence*). I asked them to take the cat to some
far-off place so that it would forget the way home
and get lost. I am waiting to see if they did.

THE WOMAN (*distracted, then suddenly paying attention to
THE OLD WOMAN*): What?

THE OLD WOMAN: I haven't slept all night because of the
cat. It keeps mewing, running, crawling under the
covers and scratching the bedclothes with its claws as
if possessed.

THE WOMAN (*still distracted*): Yes, mother?

THE OLD WOMAN: It has gotten dark. There are few
passing footsteps. You can hear a pin drop. Others
are warming themselves over a stove or drinking tea
and you have been waiting at an open window since
early morning in this cold weather. The cold stings
and pricks the face like sharp needles.

THE WOMAN (*impatiently*): I am waiting for him, mother,
waiting for him (*silence*). Let us imagine, mother,
that we sent him to buy us food for supper, for

instance, and that we are waiting for his return. I
would hear his footsteps on the paving stones in the
alley. I would recognize his footsteps (*she listens as
if hearing sounds*).

THE OLD WOMAN: Are we going to return to this subject
again? God knows where the cat has gone.

THE WOMAN: I can distinguish his footsteps among a
thousand. He leaps up the stairs, three or four at a
time. Sometimes he knocks as the half-open door,
pretending to be an outsider. "Come in, Ahmed,
come in, my dear." Then he does, taking me in his
arms and kissing me. "Are you angry, mother,
because I kissed you? I'm sorry, I'll give you the
kiss back." And he kisses me again.

THE OLD WOMAN: If his father were still alive things
wouldn't have turned out so badly. Your first-born
wouldn't have been spoiled the way he was. You
should have been firmer with him when he was a
child.

THE WOMAN: My son, Ahmed, was not a spoiled child. He
never lied, cheated, or laid hands on what was not
his. He was handsome. When he was a baby
sucking my breasts his mouth was very small and his
lips were very tender. Sometimes I was afraid that
they would be bruised if I pressed them hard, which I
did sometimes. He scratched me then. I kissed his
eyes, his mouth, his cheek, his legs, his hands. His
fist was the size of a small coin.

THE OLD WOMAN: Now you are going to start crying
again. You must leave the window and get
something to eat or you are going to collapse. You
haven't touched a piece of bread since last night.

THE WOMAN: Bread would be tasteless for me. It would
stick in my throat. How could I swallow it not
knowing whether my son is hungry or not, whether
he is feeling warm or cold. A piece of bread now

would irritate my stomach like poison.

THE OLD WOMAN: You should look in a mirror. You have become thin and your cheek-bones stick out. You look terrible.

THE WOMAN (*staring ahead as if recalling past events*): Do you remember, mother, when he got measles? His face turned blue and yellow. He didn't move. I thought he had died. I opened the door and screamed.

THE OLD WOMAN: I wasn't there then. Your sister was giving birth.

THE WOMAN: Finally he looked at me, without moving. He eyes were red and puffy. He was only a year and two months old. On that day I knew that he was kind and that he loved me, because when he saw me he smiled and his face brightened, as if he wanted to calm me with her look. I knitted woolen socks for him. (*She looks out of the window, then turns to THE OLD WOMAN.*)

THE OLD WOMAN: Let's speak frankly. Wasn't he the naughtiest boy in the neighborhood? Wasn't he a troublemaker? On his first day of school I asked him what he had done there and he answered "I bought a drink and beat up two boys."

THE WOMAN (*laughing*): What a child he was! Let us imagine, mother, that he is now visiting his aunt and we are waiting for him to return. Whenever he gets up to leave they keep him until it gets late. When he arrives he asks my sister if I am well and then sits down to read.

THE OLD WOMAN: It was those books that caused his downfall.

THE WOMAN: He was holding a book. No, no, a magazine, a green one with a glossy cover with foreign letters. His sister Ahlam was heating some tomato soup for his supper when they broke in.

THE OLD WOMAN: The kids went to get rid of the cat and they haven't come back yet. Why are they so late?

THE WOMAN: The tall man's face was yellowish, and he had evil eyes. I sensed danger from the way he pushed into the house. He looked as if he had come to take revenge on my son. "Upset this table, pull out the drawers, collect all the papers, don't leave a sheet or a book."

THE OLD WOMAN: I warned you but you wouldn't listen.

THE WOMAN: I begged them to let me talk to my son, with no success. "Let me make him a sandwich to take with him. His sister is warming up his supper. Let him put on his outdoor clothes." "No." My dear son was trying to comfort me. "I am coming back, dear mother."

THE OLD WOMAN: I beg you, drop the subject.

THE WOMAN: I wanted to buy him new pyjamas. He said "No, mother. Buy two dresses instead, one for you and one for my sister, Ahlam."

THE OLD WOMAN: She's no longer her former self. Look at her sallow face. She will kill herself over her absent brother. I wonder why the kids haven't come back. Getting rid of a cat is not all that difficult.

THE WOMAN: When I had my last illness he fed me with his own hands, making me tea with aniseed. "Just swallow this spoonful. When you get better I'll let you get married." I laughed.

THE OLD WOMAN: I asked you to make him understand what he was doing.

THE WOMAN: I did. He said "Let us look at the matter objectively."

The dark part of the stage lights up. Ahmed, a young man, appears, continuing his mother's speech. His mother looks at him dreamily while THE OLD WOMAN continues mending the shirt.

48

AHMED: The wrong side has all the luck while the right are
oppressed. People are at the end of their rope.
Everyone walks with his eyes downcast, humiliated,
frightened, frightened—as you are for me.
THE OLD WOMAN (*looking where the woman is looking.
She does not see anything, of course.*) Why don't
you eat something?
AHMED: I know how you are suffering, mother. Why do you
visit the shrines of Al Hussain and El Sayeda Zeinab?
To pray that I won't be taken away from you, that I
won't be humiliated, or have to lie out on the
pavement in winter and summer. Imagine, mother,
how many mothers suffer like you.

*The lights go out gradually, leaving that part of the
stage in darkness.*

THE WOMAN (*passionately*): I miss you so much, dear
Ahmed. I saw you yesterday in a dream.
THE OLD WOMAN (*much interested*): God bless you! What
was your dream?
THE WOMAN: I was standing in front of a big house.
Ahmed was looking out of the window of the top
story holding a book in his hand. The book was
bigger even than the window. I called him but he
didn't answer, as if he didn't hear me or see me. I
tried to climb the stairs but there seemed to be a vast
distance between him and me. He look sick, with a
pale face and sunken eyes. He remained silent, my
dear son.
THE OLD WOMAN: Don't be depressed. Dreams run
counter to reality.
THE WOMAN: When he was a boy, he used to return home
looking as if he had been rolling in the dirt. "Today
it was cold as school, mother. My classmate Ali had

49

a jacket that was hot and heavy. I gave him half my
nuts to lend it to me but after only a couple of
minutes he asked me to return the jacket to him. If
you want to keep it any longer, he said, give me the
rest of your nuts. But by that time I had finished all
my nuts."

THE OLD WOMAN: Whoever saw how diligently he
memorized his lessons would think he would turn out
to be a cabinet minister.

*MOSHUN, the younger son, a child of thirteen,
enters with torn clothes.*

THE WOMAN (*annoyed*): What's happened? Do I have to
buy you new clothes every day? Mother, come and
look. It's a tragedy.

THE OLD WOMAN: How did your clothes get torn?

MOSHEN (*reluctant and afraid*): Well . . . I fell down, on the
stairs.

THE OLD WOMAN: You should have broken your neck.

THE WOMAN: Wash up and go to bed (*MOSHEN goes out*)
and you can eat the sandwich on the table.

THE OLD WOMAN: I am very happy that they got rid of the
cat. Last night it didn't let me get any sleep at all.
You are tired. You must relax a little.

*They both go out. MOHSEN and SAWSEN, his
eleven-year-old sister, enter stealthily.*

MOHSEN: Why are you frowning? Did mother beat you?

SAWSEN: No.

MOHSEN: Then what's the matter?

SAWSEN (*angrily*): None of your business. I'm not speaking
to you.

MOHSEN: Why?

SAWSEN: You know very well why. Didn't you drive the cat

50

away?

MOHSEN: Yes I did. Grandma asked me to do it, and you ran after me and told me to leave the cat alone.

SAWSEN: Well, that's it.

MOHSEN: What reward will you give me if I show you the cat?

SAWSEN: Will you show it to me right now?

MOHSEN: Yes, right now.

SAWSEN: I'll call you a prince.

MOHSEN: And what will you give me?

SAWSEN: Everything I have.

MOHSEN: And what do you have?

SAWSEN: I have nothing. But mother will give me half a penny. I'll give that to you.

MOHSEN: And you won't go back on your word? I know you very well. If you do, I'll tell grandma what really happened. You cried and said it was cruel to chase the cat away and you refused to come with me.

SAWSEN: No. I promise. And also I'll give you . . .

MOHSEN (*interrupting her*) The pencil?

SAWSEN: Yes.

MOHSEN: The red one?

SAWSEN: No, the other one. And one-half of the eraser.

MOHSEN: You won't believe me. I took the cat across the tram line and walked until I came to the El Sayeda Fair. I stopped to watch the festivities.

SAWSEN: With the cat in your hands?

MOHSEN: I let go of it. I suddenly remember how its eyes glittered. I think it got lost. Then is went wandering among strangers, mewing and looking for me.

SAWSEN: What happened next? Tell me!

MOHSEN: I saw it coming up to me and rubbing itself on my legs. I put it up on my shoulder.

SAWSEN: Where is it now?

MOHSEN: Don't rush me. Then I remembered my grandma. I got up my courage and threw it into a walled

51

garden. It came running back to me in fear. Its body
was hot. I threw it again. It fell heavily to the
ground.

SAWSEN: How cruel you are.

MOHSEN: It stayed there, smelling the grass. It looked at me
from afar as if it understood. Then I was sorry for it.
I whistled for it to return. It looked at me as if it had
never known me. It turned its back on me and
moved off into the darkness of the park. I lost sight
of it.

SAWSEN: You are driving me crazy.

MOHSEN: I waited to hear it mew. It never did. I called it.
No response. Suddenly I heard it mew. I jumped
over the fence and caught it up in my arms.

SAWSEN: Where is it now?

MOHSEN: On the roof, all bundled up. It's cold.

SAWSEN: Let's climb up there.

MOHSEN: O.K.

*They go out. THE OLD WOMAN and THE WOMAN
enter.*

THE OLD WOMAN (*in a bad temper*): Suddenly I found the
cat in my bed, all wrapped in white. What a shock!
(*Calling loudly*) Mohsen, you naughty boy!
(*MOHSEN enters, fearfully.*)

MOHSEN: Yes, grandma.

THE OLD WOMAN: How dare you deceive me? Is this my
reward for defending you to your mother?

MOHSEN: Believe me, grandma. I took the cat and tried to
lose it. It was cold and we were in a faraway place
with no one around. I just couldn't do it.

THE OLD WOMAN: But you could let the cat keep me from
sleeping all night.

THE WOMAN: Well, mother, what if we let the cat stay in
the house?

52

THE OLD WOMAN (*astonished*): What's that? Let the cat stay in the house?

THE WOMAN: Yes, mother. It's a living soul. Don't disappoint the kids.

THE OLD WOMAN: I'll break their necks. Where's that damned Swasen?

THE WOMAN: She's inside.

MOHSEN and THE OLD WOMAN exit. THE WOMAN is left alone. A plover is heard singing outside.

THE WOMAN: Even the plover prays to God. Please, God, preserve our homes from strangers who come to take a son away from his mother. Death is enough to separate us.

A radio is heard outside.

THE RADIO: The News Bulletin.

THE MOTHER (*sarcastically*): What educated voices we hear. My soon was education. He studied politics.

THE RADIO: These are the top stories.

THE MOTHER (*turning the radio down*): Bloody liar. Just like the newspapers. It's all fiction. What age do we live in? It's like old times. My son was carried off in front of me and his beloved sister. He didn't steal anything or cheat anyone or lie to anyone. (*She calms down a little. THE OLD WOMAN enters.*)

THE OLD WOMAN: I gave them a real beating.

THE WOMAN: What saddens me the most, mother, is that they took away my son in full view of the neighbors with the shoulder of his pyjamas worn out. What a same! (*Gently*) Ahmed, I asked you to buy new pyjamas, but you refused. You shouldn't have refused, my son. (*She goes to the window and looks*

53

out, waiting for the return of her absent son.)

Curtain

The Nightmare

by Lenin El-Ramly

translated by Marvin Carlson and Wagdi Zeid

The Nightmare

Lenin El-Ramly

Time: Neutral

Place: At the rear of the stage, an enormous spider web. Behind, a high window. In front, a wall clock, a small table with a telephone, sofa, a rocking chair with a writing tablet on it which is blank, (a pedestal with a simple empty frame,) an old coat-rack on which are hanging a dressing gown and nightcap, on the non-existent wall, a frame with a photo of the grand-father in a tarboosh, a mourning band on the corner. No doors, but one can imagine exits toward the interior and exterior of the house.

Note: The characters scarcely speak to each other, except occasionally the maid. Almost all the father's words are addressed to the audience. The grandfather speaks from the photo, or moves out from it and then returns to his frozen position. All the characters perform their parts seriously even if their words have comic overtones.

THE FATHER sits on a chair, his face hidden behind his newspaper. THE MAID moves silently in the background, coming and going as if she is organizing the place.

THE FATHER: (*turning the page without looking at THE MAID*): Do your work well.

THE MOTHER comes from within, pushing a rolling armchair on which THE YOUNG MAN is seated. She stops and remains without moving. From time to time, she makes a half-step with her right foot, then one with her left foot, then stops again, as if she were a pawn on the chessboard.

THE MOTHER: My son!

*THE YOUNG MAN turns his armchair, offering his back
to the audience. THE SISTER comes from within. In her
hurry, she trips over her long white robe. She wears a
violet shawl; when she removes it, her dress is seen to be
cut low in the back. She stops by the telephone, waits,
then paces back and forth anxiously, as if waiting for it to
ring. The telephone rings. THE SISTER looks at the
telephone, then backs away slowly, moving fearfully away
from it until the ringing stops.*

THE MOTHER: My daughter!

*THE SISTER picks up her knitting from the chair next to
the telephone. She sits and begins to knit. THE YOUNG
MAN turns completely around on the armchair.*

THE SISTER: (*without looking up from her knitting*) Are you
there?
THE YOUNG MAN: (*stopping his turning*) No . . . Yes.
THE MOTHER: (*making a half step*) Are you going out?
THE YOUNG MAN: (*in the same tone*) Yes . . . No.

A long moment of silence.

THE YOUNG MAN: Did anyone ask for me?
THE SISTER: (*she stops knitting and looks fixedly in front of
her. A ball of yarn falls and rolls across the floor. As if
insulting the young man*) No one!

Music.

THE YOUNG MAN: (*pushes the armchair up to the wall and
looks out from behind it*) I'm busy. (*He reflects a
moment, then nonchalantly traces circles in the air.*) I am
an engineer. I can build a house . . . a new house . . . a
big house . . .

THE SISTER lifts the telephone receiver. THE
BROTHER arrives from outside.

THE SISTER: (*leaping back, as if caught in some humiliating act*) My brother!

THE BROTHER: (*He looks around at them all and then speaks in a solemn tone*) I am going there and not coming back! (*He moves to the edge of the group and pays no attention to them.*) I am gone.

THE FATHER: Thirty years he wasted in school.

THE MOTHER: My dear one!

THE YOUNG MAN repeats a movement of crossing out and beginning over again.

THE FATHER: Paper . . . book . . . words . . . ink . . . without result.

THE MOTHER: My dear one!

THE FATHER: I gave up my life for him. Provided him with all his toys. His doll and his horse. His bibs and his rattles. His model train and his seesaw. His clown hat and whistle. All his toys.

THE MOTHER: My dear one!

THE FATHER: And he thinks he is planning the world.

THE YOUNG MAN: I am certain that something will happen.

THE MAID: (*coming in with a box of cigars, handing them out*) It was a boy . . . or perhaps a girl . . .no, it was a boy.

THE MOTHER: Listen to the words of your father. And listen to the words of your mother.

THE GRANDFATHER: Do not listen to what is said in books . . . listen to the what the teacher says in class.

THE FATHER: Listen to "The Voice of the Arabs" . . . Don't listen to CNN.

THE YOUNG MAN: Something is going to happen.

THE MOTHER: Oh, God, may my boy grow up to become a general, but may there be no wars.

59

THE FATHER: My son should be like Gamal Abdul Nassar . . at least like Abdul Nassar . . . or maybe King Farouk.

The clock strikes several times. THE YOUNG MAN 's pen stops in his hand. His face contracts. His body shakes with silent, broken sobs.)

THE MOTHER: *(approaching a step, with appre-hension)* My son.

THE YOUNG MAN breaks into sobs that rise in tone.

THE GRANDFATHER: *(in his picture frame)* Who is it?
THE SISTER: *(to herself)* No one at all.
THE MOTHER: Oh, my son. He is feverish.
THE GRANDFATHER: Feed him.
THE MOTHER: Take this nipple . . . Go to sleep, now.
THE YOUNG MAN: Thirsty . . .
THE MAID: "Jack and Jill went up the hill, to get a drink of water . . ."
THE GRANDFATHER: "The child fell down . . ."
THE MAID: But his father picked him up.
THE MOTHER: Poor child, his crown is broken.
THE FATHER: Life has become difficult. I have to travel, get money, spend it on him. *(He gets up and leaves.)*
THE YOUNG MAN: Wake me up early. I have an important appointment. I have to find myself and give myself a good talking to.
THE MOTHER: May God put honest people in your path, my dearest.
THE SISTER: You will find nothing, even if you go..
THE MAID: *(sweeping and moving the dust in their direction. She finishes her work and sits down near THE SISTER)* At your service, sir. At your service, madam.
THE BROTHER: *(turning and going to his sister's side)* I have come back and I need to sleep.

60

THE MAID. At your service, sir (*she starts to stand up*)
THE SISTER: You criminal! You low, base creature! You
   weak vessel! You inferior being! You awkward dolt!
THE MAID: My master, mistress (*bending her head and
   sitting down again*).
THE BROTHER: I am going to sleep.
THE MAID: My mistress, master.
THE SISTER: Outcast! Peasant! Beggar! Monster! Maid!
THE BROTHER: Go away.
THE MAID: (*recovering*) At your service, master. (*The
   brother goes offstage and the maid follows him*).
THE SISTER: (*weeping*) You are a degenerate, you flirt with
   boys, you have no morals.
THE YOUNG MAN: (*as if regaining consciousness*) It was a
   horrible nightmare. I couldn't breathe.
THE MOTHER: What was it?
THE YOUNG MAN: (*getting up and walking to the sofa*) I
   dreamed I was alive.
THE MOTHER: (*regretfully*) You were sleeping in the open
   air.
THE YOUNG MAN: (*agitatedly*) It was not in the open air . .
   . I . . . (*He loses courage as he speaks and falls silent*)
THE MOTHER: Have a little rice and mouloukhia.
THE YOUNG MAN: Why am I unable to speak?
THE MOTHER: Have a little bread and gumbo.
THE YOUNG MAN: There is speech stirring within me . . . I
   am going to explode.

Music.

THE SISTER: (*She pulls sharply at the ball of yarn, which
   rolls away. She gets up and crawls after it on all fours.*)
THE YOUNG MAN: (*seriously, but to himself*) Something is
   about to happen.

The telephone rings.

THE SISTER: (*She stops crawling about and looks briefly in its direction. Then she gets up and moves toward the telephone, but stops about a meter away from it. She reaches toward it, then pulls it toward her and bites it.*)

The telephone stops ringing. After a moment, THE SISTER goes toward the telephone on tiptoe and listens to the receiver.

THE GRANDFATHER: (*in his frame*) Who is it?
THE SISTER: (*putting down the receiver and turning toward him*). No one.

The telephone rings again. THE SISTER, as if she did not hear, she goes away from it. THE YOUNG MAN moves back and forth and then stops in front of the picture, looking at it. The clock strikes. THE YOUNG MAN tries to speak. He presses his hand to his chest as if to point to himself, but he remains silent.

THE MOTHER: (*sorrowfully and anxiously*) My son!
THE YOUNG MAN: Today I am thirty years old.
THE GRANDFATHER: Wean him!

THE YOUNG MAN emits a long, fearful cry.   Music.

THE MOTHER: What do you feel, my dear?
THE YOUNG MAN: (*as if suffering*) I feel nothing.
THE GRANDFATHER: "Spare the rod and spoil the child."
THE FATHER: God have mercy on you, father.
THE GRANDFATHER: And good fortune to you.
THE YOUNG MAN: The doctor wrote me a prescrip-tion.
THE SISTER: I am a doctor, but I can't examine men.
THE YOUNG MAN: The doctor told me to think three times a day before eating.
THE MOTHER: Eat humble pie and drink deep ere you

62

depart.

THE YOUNG MAN: I have to think.

THE MOTHER: Others envy him.

THE GRANDFATHER: Have him exorcised.

THE MAID: (*burning incense*) I am exorcising you from all those who envy you, from all your rivals. First . .

THE YOUNG MAN: (*pacing about as the incense burns*) I am thinking.

THE MAID: And second . . .

THE YOUNG MAN: I am thinking.

THE MAID: And third . . .

THE MOTHER: (*sticking pins in a doll*) You are free from the eye of your neighbor and the eye of your friends and the eye of your sister and the eye of your mother, my dear son, and the eye of all those who have looked upon you without giving you their blessing.

THE YOUNG MAN: (*as if discovering something*) I am thinking.

THE MOTHER: (*agitated*). He has grown up!

THE GRANDFATHER: Cleanse him.

THE MAID: (*wildly*) Cast salt for him seven times, mother of the circumcised, enter a holy shrine and light seven candles.

THE SISTER: "Don't cry, little bridegroom , this too shall pass."

THE GRANDFATHER: "And that's true, too."

THE YOUNG MAN: Shut up so that I can think.

A moment of silence.

THE YOUNG MAN: " To be or not to be" . . . That is the joke.

THE MOTHER: My child!

THE GRANDFATHER: Summon up a spirit.

THE MAID: Hear ye! Hear ye! A child is missing!.

THE YOUNG MAN: "To be or not to be" . . . That is the

question.

MOTHER: He is lost.

THE YOUNG MAN: Which of these cases is more profitable for the soul?

Which of these profits is more suitable for wearing?

Which of these suits is closer to love?

Which of these loves is better for the stud?

Which of these studs is more suited to solitude?

Which of these solitudes is more studded with sense?

Which of these senses is more suited for nonsense?

Which of these whiches . . .

THE SISTER: *(goes in the direction he is pointing, listens to him, then stops and whispers)* A man.

THE MAID: The master is returning.

THE YOUNG MAN: My father *(he comes back with a heavy tread, then sits on the rolling chair).*

THE FATHER enters from outside with a suitcase.

THE FATHER: Thanks be to God for my safe return. I couldn't live in the Gulf States. After sixteen years I swear I couldn't remain another day.

THE MAID: Master, oh, master. *(She brings to him his dressing gown from the coat rack, takes off his jacket and hangs it up on the coat rack, then goes to sit at THE SISTER's feet.)*

THE FATHER *(adjusts his dressing gown, then takes off his mustache and puts it in his pocket and sits down in the rocking chair.)* I brought some gifts with me. Rosaries and pilgrim's hats for my friends, companions and loved ones . . . Actually I bought them in the Cairo bazaar. You are quite under-developed here. While there, in the Gulf, we have Egyptian TV series before you do.

THE YOUNG MAN: A horrible nightmare *(He moves as if to get up but he is unsuccessful and falls back in his chair a second time.)*

64

THE FATHER: A foolish folly.

THE MOTHER: (*quickly*) My dear one!

THE YOUNG MAN: I have to be there because some-thing is going to happen. I have to know what it is.

THE BROTHER: (*He appears from within, packing a sport suitcase*) I am going to the match and I won't come back until we win. And if we win the cup . . . I will drink (*He takes a cup from the suitcase, drinks from it, and leaves.*)

THE YOUNG MAN: (*He looks around himself for something, then cries out*) A pencil!

THE MAID: (*not moving*) At your service, sir. At your service, madam.

THE YOUNG MAN: (*He rises, casts a glance among them and says, in a threatening tone*) Who has taken the pencil?

THE MOTHER: My son!

THE SISTER: No one.

THE YOUNG MAN: (*He steps back as if to avoid falling into a trap*) You are all against me.

THE SISTER: (*She laughs a long and nervous, a crudely seductive laugh*)

THE YOUNG MAN: Give me my pencil!

THE SISTER: (*She goes up to him and holds out her lipstick.*)

THE YOUNG MAN: That won't write!

THE SISTER: It will write!

THE YOUNG MAN: (*doubtfully*) It won't write.

THE SISTER: It will write (*She draws a red line on his cheeks and forehead, then draws a red x on the front of his white shirt, then steps back and observes him.*)

THE YOUNG MAN: The pencil, rabble! (*He finds the pencil in the pocket of his shirt, seizes it as if it were a knife, and looks around himself in astonishment.*) I must do something new.

THE MOTHER: Do it, my dear.

THE YOUNG MAN lifts up the pencil and stabs himself

with it. THE MOTHER put the pencil on the chair and pushes him away.

THE FATHER: A corrupted generation . . . degenerate . . . effeminate. I can eat two kilos of kafta and kebob all by myself.

THE YOUNG MAN: Oh!

THE MOTHER: My son is tired.

THE GRANDFATHER: Get him married.

Suddenly THE YOUNG WOMAN enters from the rear and approaches THE YOUNG MAN.

THE MAID: (*dancing and singing*) " Mine eyes have seen the glory of the coming of the Lord; He is stamping out the vintage where the grapes of wrath are stored . . . "

THE YOUNG WOMAN: (*tenderly*) I want nothing from you.

THE YOUNG MAN: (*without looking at her*) You want everything . . .

THE YOUNG WOMAN: I want you, yourself.

THE YOUNG MAN: (*finishing his sentence*) . . . except the most important thing.

THE YOUNG WOMAN: I am afraid.

THE SISTER: Go. Let's go.

THE FATHER: He is drowning in an inch of water.

THE MOTHER: It is crowded outside, my son.

THE YOUNG MAN: And I am crowded within me, also.

THE GRANDFATHER: Eat, walk about, and marry four times.

THE YOUNG MAN: I will build a house. A grand house. A house everyone will talk about. A house that will stand the test of time.

THE YOUNG WOMAN: I will wait for you. (*She disappears.*)

THE MAID: (*returning to her sweeping*) At your service, sir. At your service.

66

THE FATHER: (*bouncing on his chair after each phrase*)
When I was small I took first place. My shoes were
always clean and polished, and my nails trimmed. I was
very clever. I bought cheap and sold high. I was content
with my lot. I exercised. All my friends loved me. I
prospered from the beginning by respecting my father.
THE GRANDFATHER: "Strike the tethered animal. This
will frighten the free one."
THE FATHER: (*speaking to his picture*) God have mercy on
you, father.
THE GRANDFATHER: And good fortune to you.
THE MAID: All this comes from the evil spirits. My God
protect us from them. (*She sings the zar music of
exorcism, followed by the others.*)
THE YOUNG MAN: I am going to paint a picture.
THE MOTHER: Paint, my dear.
THE YOUNG MAN: I am going to paint a picture. I painted
one already and called it "The Mona Lisa."
THE FATHER: All this will end up in the garbage.
THE MOTHER: My dear one.

(*THE MAID appears to report the news and then
disappears again.*)

THE MAID: Have you read the newspapers?
THE SISTER: (*interested*) Look at Virgo.
THE FATHER (*picking up a newspaper and reading from it*)
Good news! You will conceive this month!
THE MAID: The minister was killed in the street. (*She
disappears.*)
THE GRANDFATHER: Oh, God! Tombs will become
expensive.
THE SISTER: I am a doctor. The person killed, after being
killed, dies.
THE FATHER: I refuse to be a minister, as long as they don't
ask me.

THE MAID: (*appearing and addressing THE FATHER*)
Master . . . your mother has been caught begging (*she disappears*).

THE FATHER: (*balancing on his chair*) I donated to Bosnia-Herzegovnia.

THE GRANDFATHER: I will divorce her. She has been disobedient.

THE SISTER: No one. I am a doctor.

THE YOUNG MAN: I am going to write a letter.

THE MOTHER: Write, dear.

THE MAID (*appearing and addressing THE FATHER*)
Master . . . your sister has been caught in a house of ill fame.

THE FATHER: She is not my full sister.

THE SISTER: My dear aunt.

THE GRANDFATHER: I was married to her mother secretly. She was limited in knowledge.

THE FATHER: God have mercy on you, father.

THE GRANDFATHER: And good fortune to you.

THE YOUNG MAN: I am going to write to . . . to . . .

THE SISTER: (*She grabs at the telephone nervously, then put down the receiver, giving up, and moves away.*)

THE YOUNG MAN: (*An idea comes to him.*) I will write a letter to humanity!

THE MAID: (*appearing*) An earthquake hit across the street and the house beside us collapsed.(*She disappears.*)

THE SISTER: (*shrieking*) I am a doctor, you a servant, a peasant, a missing person, a reject, a fool, a degenerate.

THE FATHER: (*taking a sack from his valise and swallowing its contents voraciously*) Out there in the Gulf States, not a single house has collapsed.

THE YOUNG MAN: Dear humanity! How are you and how are all the family . . . ?

THE MAID: (*appearing*) There is no water in the pipes (*She disappears*).

THE YOUNG MAN: You cowardly mice, you, rats, rise up

against the fat cats. If you work together, you can place a bell around their necks, and when they get close to you, you can get away, before you are eaten.

THE FATHER belches loudly.

THE MAID: (*appearing*) The sewers are overflowing.
THE YOUNG MAN: I am thirsty.
THE MAID: At your service, master (*she disappears*).
THE MOTHER: (I suckled him, two years, three years, four years, until he was weaned. He went through thousands of cartons of milk.

THE FATHER, having finished eating, im-mediately falls asleep.

THE YOUNG MAN: I am thirsty.
THE MAID: (*She enters with a glass of water, but pours it over THE SISTER, who remains unmoving*) To your health!

THE BROTHER comes in from outside and goes toward the interior.

THE BROTHER: We took our revenge. We beat the referee.
THE MAID: Yes, sir. (*She moves behind THE BROTHER to go inside.*)
THE SISTER: (*weeping*) You are a degenerate. You flirt with boys. You have no morals.
THE YOUNG MAN: I have made a discovery.
THE MOTHER: Congratulations, my dear!
THE YOUNG MAN: All bodies lifted into space will fall back, all matter and energy is conserved,. and nothing is created from nothing.

THE FATHER, still sleeping, snores.

THE MOTHER: Bless you, my dear!

THE MAID appears, seven months pregnant.

THE MAID: I have kneaded the dough and baked it, and
    peeled the onions and collected and chopped the
    vegetables, and cooked them, and cleaned the tiles and
    dried them, and done the laundry and spread it out to dry
    and hung it up. Have I served my time?
THE SISTER: Leave us.

*THE MAID sits down at THE SISTER's feet, combs her
hair and hums a familiar folk tune. THE BROTHER
appears and crosses toward the outside.*

THE BROTHER: I am going to get drunk and I have to sleep
    outside.
THE YOUNG MAN: I am going to invent something.
THE MOTHER: (*mournfully*) You are wearing yourself out,
    dear.
THE YOUNG MAN: What shall I invent? What shall I
    invent? Oh! I will invent something for the kitchen! A
    tin cabinet, yes, of tin. With a little lamp in it. When it is
    plugged it, it lights up the cabinet. And inside shelves to
    pull out and on them foods and glasses. Every day you
    buy a block of ice and put in on a platform on top and this
    preserves the food and drinks by cooling them. I will call
    this invention a refrigerator. No, a "fridge" would be
    better.
THE SISTER: (*kicking THE MAID in the back*) Dog! Wretch!
    Good for nothing!
THE MAID: (*weeping and crying out while moving away
    awkwardly, singing seductively* "Whiter than snow . . .
    whiter than snow . . . wash me and I shall be whiter than
    snow."
THE YOUNG MAN: I am going to compose something.

70

THE MOTHER: Compose, dear!
THE YOUNG MAN: (*He thinks deeply, then writes*) I have
   composed something. Be silent! Listen!
THE MOTHER: Hush!

*THE YOUNG MAN raises his hand as if he were holding
a conductor's baton and gestures with it as we hear the
beginning of a classical symphony, then it changes to a
banal, local, cheap song.*

THE GRANDFATHER: Music is not forbidden. But it is not
   approved, either.
THE FATHER: (*waking up briefly*) Over in the Gulf States
   there in no music, but there is . . . (*then he goes back to
   sleep and snores*).

THE MAID goes out.

THE YOUNG MAN: I will become a philosopher. I must
   utter some maxim.
THE MOTHER: Speak, dear.
THE GRANDFATHER: "If you fear the Master, then keep
   silent."
THE YOUNG MAN: (*cautiously*) I must utter some maxim. I
   must utter some maxim.
THE GRANDFATHER: "Walk gently, and don't cross the
   boundaries."

THE FATHER snores.

THE MOTHER: Oh, my son!
THE YOUNG MAN: I must utter some maxim.
THE GRANDFATHER: "When entering a house, leave a trail
   of thread."
THE YOUNG MAN: I must utter some maxim. (*As if
   discovering it.*) I speak . . . I speak . . . therefore I am.

71

THE FATHER snores loudly.

THE MOTHER: Eat butter and blancmange.

THE YOUNG MAN: (*desperately*) I must become progressive.

THE MOTHER: Move forward, my son.

THE YOUNG MAN: (*with determination*) I must become the first, the first in line, ahead of everyone.

THE MOTHER: Get up, my son, get up, wash your face, have some breakfast, and emigrate.

THE FATHER: (*awakening and raising his head*) Out there in the Gulf States . . . (*He yawns and goes back to sleep.*)

THE MAID: (*entering*) He will contribute to the new order.

THE YOUNG MAN: I have a project for a house better than anyone else's.

THE YOUNG WOMAN: (*entering*) You are very far away, my dear.

THE YOUNG MAN moves away and hides behind the coat rack.

THE YOUNG WOMAN: (*looking for him*) Come closer.

THE MOTHER: Get married, dear.

THE YOUNG MAN: (*He appears behind the young woman and guides her.*) I betrayed you.

THE YOUNG WOMAN: (*turning to him*) Was she more beautiful than I?

THE YOUNG MAN: Much.

THE YOUNG WOMAN: (*moving to the rear*) You met her often?

THE YOUNG MAN: I was always with her.

THE MOTHER: Get married, dear. I want to see you married and divorced before I die.

THE YOUNG WOMAN: Assure me that you will no longer think about her.

THE YOUNG MAN: I am going to meet her.

THE YOUNG WOMAN: Traitor! Cheat!

THE YOUNG MAN: I have betrayed you.

THE YOUNG WOMAN: Wretch! Scoundrel!

THE MOTHER: Before I die I want to see you married and widowed.

THE GRANDFATHER: Women are deficient in reason and religion. Get married.

THE SISTER: All men are filth and all women are impure.

THE BROTHER comes in from outside and crosses to go inside.

THE BROTHER: (*dryly*) The maid has run away.

THE SISTER: (*frightened*) With the flatiron? The traitress, seducer of men . . . shameless hussy!

THE FATHER: (*rising, angrily*) We must call the police (*He sits down again*).

THE BROTHER enters from inside and crosses to go out.

THE BROTHER: (*He is wearing a galabieh and wooden clogs and has a beard*) I am going to the mosque and will not return.

THE GRANDFATHER: God is great!

THE SISTER: (*runs two steps after him and then returns*) No one.

THE YOUNG WOMAN: I am going away.

THE YOUNG MAN: (*frightened*) Don't leave me.

THE YOUNG WOMAN: Go to her.

THE YOUNG MAN: I can't find her.

THE YOUNG WOMAN: (*gloating*) She left you?

THE FATHER: You lose everything you want.

THE YOUNG MAN: I have never seen her in my life.

THE YOUNG WOMAN: She is playing with you.

THE YOUNG MAN: I have wandered everywhere looking for her. I didn't find her anywhere.

THE YOUNG WOMAN: (*shaking him by the shoulders*) And
I? . . . And I? . . . And I?
THE SISTER: And I?
THE YOUNG MAN: I am betraying her with you.
THE YOUNG WOMAN: (*she starts to move away*) Traitor!
THE YOUNG MAN: (*seizing her hand*) Don't leave me.
THE MOTHER: (*groping her way as if blind*) I am beside
you, my dear.
THE YOUNG MAN: In the night . . I am afraid of the coat
rack.
THE FATHER: He's afraid of his own shadow.
THE MOTHER: My dear one.
THE YOUNG WOMAN: My dear heart (*She embraces and
caresses him compassionately*).

Music. THE BROTHER comes in from outside, slowly.

THE BROTHER: (*taking off his mustache, then, in a decisive
tone*) I found my friends.
THE FATHER: Nobody can defeat me. I have never been
defeated. My manager himself couldn't defeat me. He
tried once, twice, three times, ten times. He wanted
desperately to humiliate me, but he couldn't. Every time
it was I who defeated him. Every time we played I won.
I checkmated him.
THE YOUNG MAN: (*He remains lost in his thoughts,
stretching out his arms toward the window*) Come!
THE YOUNG WOMAN: (*She moves around him to attract
his attention*) Look at me. Think about me. Search for
me.
THE SISTER: (*lifting the receiver of the telephone*) No one.
THE YOUNG WOMAN: I am going away.
THE YOUNG MAN: (*cooly*) Leave me.
THE YOUNG WOMAN: Oh, my beloved.
THE MOTHER: Oh, my son.
THE SISTER: My son, my love, my dear, my heart, my eyes.

74

When will I give birth to you?

THE YOUNG MAN: Something must happen.

THE MOTHER: (*singing to him in a low voice*) "Bye, baby bunting, Daddy's gone a-hunting. . ."

THE BROTHER: Did someone call me?

Silence.

THE SISTER: No one.

THE FATHER laughs suddenly and points at something on the floor.

THE YOUNG WOMAN: (*looking at the floor*) A cockroach has fallen on his back.

THE MOTHER: (*weeping and covering her face*) My dear!

THE SISTER: (*following the cockroach*) It is raising up its feet.

THE YOUNG WOMAN: It's twitching.

THE GRANDFATHER: Forward march, Rommel!

THE SISTER: (*to THE BROTHER*) The cockroach, do you see it?

THE YOUNG MAN: It's going to turn over by itself.

THE FATHER: It's not going to get up.

THE YOUNG WOMAN: It's moving. It's crawling on its back.

THE SISTER: I'm a doctor but I don't examine men.

THE FATHER: It is going to die alone.

THE MOTHER: My dear!

THE FATHER: (*balancing on his chair*) I was never defeated in sports.

THE YOUNG WOMAN: (*going toward THE BROTHER*) No use.

THE BROTHER: No interest.

THE SISTER: (*She returns, sits, and takes up her knitting*) No one.

THE YOUNG MAN: (*He opens his eyes suddenly and cries out*) A frightful dream, a terrifying nightmare!
THE MOTHER: (*frightened*) My son!
THE YOUNG MAN: I dreamed that I was walking on legs.
THE MOTHER: Your fate, my son.

The clock strikes without stopping, the sound gradually getting louder until it resembles a heavy hammering. Then it changes to the sound like winches lifting the stones of ruined houses. The light gradually fades.

THE YOUNG MAN: (*looking at his watch. He gets up, exhausted but determined. He forces himself to move, with dragging steps.*) I finished the new building . . . here it is . . . "except the Lord build a house, they labor in vain that build it." (*Then he sits on the revolving chair and turns himself around on it.*) Something should happen. Something should happen. And I have to be there to know what is going to happen.

All continue to repeat the same movements for a time while the stage slowly darkens. THE BROTHER stands with his back to the audience, his arms behind him. THE SISTER continues to knit. THE FATHER balances on his chair eating some lettuce that he has cut up. THE GRAND-FATHER in his picture frame twirls his mustache.

The CURTAIN falls.

Contemporary Egyptian Drama in English: Bibliography

General Studies

Allen, Roger, "Drama and Audience: The Case of Arabic Theater," *Theater 3* 6 (1989), 25-54.

Atiyeh, George, "*Oedipus Rex* in Modern Arabic Literature," in Michael Ferdinandy Festschrift, *Uberlieferung und Auftrag*. Pressler: Wies-baden, 1972, 134-47.

Badawi, M.M., "Arabic Drama and Politics Since the Fifties," in *Gesellschaftlicher Umbruch und Historie im Zeitgenössischen Drama der Islamischen Welt*, ed. J.C. Bürgel, Beirut, 1995, pp. 1-21.

Cachia, Pierre, *An Overview of Modern Arabic Literature*.Edinburgh University, 1990. Chaps. 7, "The Theatrical Movement of the Arabs," 9, "Idealism and Identity: The Case of Tawfīq al-Hakim," and 10, "Unwritten Arabic Fiction and Drama."

Jayyusi, Salma and Roger Allen, *Modern Arabic Drama: An Anthology*. Indiana University, 1995.

Machut-Mendecka, Ewa, "Concepts of History and Society in Modern Arabic Drama" 179-89.

-----------, "The Concept of Time in Arabic Drama," *Rocznik Orientalistyczny* (Warsaw) 1 (1995): 53-59.

-----------, "Development Identity of Arabic Drama," *Africana Bull.* (Warsaw) 39 (1991), 63-75.

Al-Mubarak, Khalid, *Arabic Drama: A Critical Introduction*. Khartoum University, 1986.

Al-Ra'i, Ali, "Arabic Drama Since the Thirties," Chapter 10 in *The Cambridge History of Arabic Literature: Modern Arabic Literature*. Cambridge, 1992.

Al-Ra'i, Ali, "Some Aspects of Modern Arabic Drama," in *Studies in Modern Arabic Literature*, ed. R.C. Ostle. Warminster: Aris and Phillips, 1975, pp. 166-78.

Al-Shetawi, Mahmoud, "The Arab-West Conflict as
    Represented in Arabic Drama, *WLT*, 61,1 (Winter, 1987),
    46-49.
Stetkevych, J., "Classical Arabic on Stage," in *Studies in
    Modern Arabic Literature*, 152-66.
The World Encyclopedia of Contemporary Theatre, Volume 4,
    "The Arab World–Egypt," pp. 70-100

Critical and Historical Studies of Contemporary Egyptian Theatre

Abou-Saif, L. "Creating a Theatre of the Poor at Wekalat al-Ghouri in Cairo," *Arab Cultural Scene*, 1982, 100-104.

Allen, Roger, "The Artistry of Yusuf Idris," *WLT*, 55,1 (Winter, 1981), 43-47.

----------. "Egyptian Drama after the Revolution," *Edebiyat*, 4,1 (1979), 97-134.

----------. "Egyptian Drama and Fiction in the 1970s,: *Edebiyat*, 1 (1976), 219-34.

Awad, Louis, "Problems of the Egyptian Theatre," in *Studies in Modern Arabic Literature*, ed. R.C. Ostle, Warminster, 1975, 179-93.

Badaur, Muhammad. *Modern Arabic Drama in Egypt.* Cambridge, 1987.

Badawi, M.M., *Modern Arabic Drama in Egypt*, Cambridge, 1987.

Brown, Irving, "The Effervescent Egyptian Theatre," *Theatre Annual* 21 (1964): 57-68.

Gad, Leila, "The Puppet Theatre in Cairo, *World Theatre* 14:5 (1965)452-3.

Hammouda, Abdel-Azia, "Modem Egyptian Theatre: Three Major Dramatists," *WLT*, 53,4 (Autumn, 1979), 601-5.

El-Lozy, Mahmoud, "Brecht and the Egyptian Political Theatre," *Alif*, 10 (1990): 56-73.

----------, "Censoring the Censor: The Politics of Satire in Nu'man Ashur's *Sima Awanta*," *Theatre Three* (fall, 1989), 31-46.

Machuat-Mendecka, Ewa, "Social Changes in Egyptian Realistic Drama," *Africana Eulletin* (Warsaw) 30 (1981), 147-58.

----------, "European and Arab Elements in Egyptian Drama," *Africana Bulletin* (Warsaw) 29 (1980), 109-21.

Omotoso, Kole, "Arabic Drama and Islamic Belief-System in Egypt," *African Literature Today* 8 (1976): 99-105.

Ramadan, Abdel, "Egypt's Theatre is International" *UN World* 5 (March, 1951), 61-2.

Sarhan, Samir, "The Zar Beat," *The Drama Review* 25 (winter, 1981), 19-24

Semaan, Khalil I. "Drama as a Vehicle of Protest in Nasir's Egypt," *International Journal of Middle Eastern Studies*, 10 (1979):49-53.

Selaiha, Nehad, *Egyptian Theatre: A Diary 1990-1992* GEBO: 1993

----------, "Introduction" to Sabur, *Now the King is Dead*, 1-16.

Wahab, Farouk, "Introduction," to *Modern Egyptian Drama*. Bibliotheca Islamica: Minneapolis, 1974.

English Translations of Contemporary Egyptian Plays (since 1955)

Ashoor, Nomann, *Give Us Our Money Back* (1958), Elias Publishing, Cairo, 1994.

----------, *The House of Al-Dughry* (1963),Ministry of Culture Press, Cairo, 1998

Basheer, Abdallah, *When the Eagle Dreams* (1955). G.E.B.O: Cairo, 1996.

El-Deweri Raafat, *Cat with Seven Lives, an Egyptian Ritual Folkloric Drama*. G.E.B.O.: Cairo, 1988.

Diab, Mahmoud, *The Storm* (1954). *The Drama.*

----------, *Strangers Don't Drink Coffee* in the anthology *Modern Arabic Drama.*

----------, *Gate to Conquest* (1971) Ministry of Culture, 1998.

Enani, Mohamad, *The Prisoner and the Jailor, The Lake, Two Friends* (all 1980). G.E.B.O.: Cairo, 1989.

Farag, Alfred, *Al-Zeer Salim*, available in MS

----------, *Ali Janah Al-Tabrizi and his Servant Quffa* in the anthology *Modern Arabic Drama.* Also individual printing.

----------, *Marriage by Decree Nisi* G.E.B.O., Cairo, 1992

----------, *The Trap*, in the anthology *Egyptian One-Act Plays.*

----------, *The Stranger* , available in MS

----------, *The Person* (1989), available in MS

El Ghamry, Atef, *House of Principles,* available in MS.

----------, *The Man at the Top,* available in MS

Guwaida, Farooq, *Blood Stains on the Veils of the Kaaba,* G.E.B.O.: Cairo, 1996

Hakim, Shawki Abdel, *Hassan end Naima* (1965). In anthology *The Drama.*

Al-Hakim, Tawfiq,*Fate of a Cockroach* (1966) in *Fate of a Cockroach and Other Plays* Three Continents: Boulder, 1994.

----------, *Food for the Millions* (1963). *Plays, Prefaces and Postscripts of Tawfiq Al-Hakim.* 2 vol. (henceforth *PPP*).

Three Continents: Boulder, CO, 1981), vol.1. *PPP*, vol.2.

----------, *Incrimination* (1966). *PPP*,

----------, *Not a Thing Out of Place* (1966) in *Fate of a Cockroach.*

----------, *Poet on the Moon* (1972). *PPP*, vol.2.

----------. *Princess Sunshine* (1965). *PPP*,

----------, *The Sultan's Dilemma* (1960) in *Fate of a Cockroach.*

----------, *Tender Hands* (1954). *PPP*, vol.2.

----------, *The Tree Climber* (1962) Oxford University, 1966.

----------, *Voyage to Tomorrow* (1957). *PPP*, vol. 2

Idris, Youssef, *Flipflap and His Master* (1964). *The Drama.*

Ismail, Izz El-Din, *The Trial of an Unknown Man* (1960s), G.E.B.O.,: Cairo, 1985

Juwayda, Faruq, *Blood Stains.* G.E.B.O.: Cairo, 1996.

----------, *The Fall of Cordova.* G.E.B.O.: Cairo, 1988.

Kamil, Farid, *The Interrogation*, in *Egyptian One-Act Plays.*

Khorshid, Farouk, *The Wines of Babylon* (1967). *The Drama.*

Mahfuz, Najib, *The Chase* (1973),*Mundus Artium* 10,1(1977):134-62.

----------, *Harassment* (1972), *JAL* 9 (1978): 105-37.

Maqsood, Gamal Abdel, *The Man Who Ate a Goose* (1985). G.E.B.O.: Cairo, 1991.

Radwan, Fathi, *A God in Spite of Himself, JAL* 10 (1974):108-26.

El-Ramly, Lenin, *In Plain Arabic* (1991), American U Press, 1994.

----------. *A Point of View,* Ministry of Culture press, 1998

Romane, Mikhail, *The Newcomer* (1967). *The Drama.*

Rushdy, Rashad, *In the Ladies' Compartment, JAL* 2 (1971): 92-97.

----------, *A Journey Outside the Wall* (1963) in *Modern Egyptian Drama.*

Al-Sabur, Salah Abd, *Murder in Baghdad* (1964). Brill:Leiden,1972.

----------, *Night Traveler* (1969) in *Modern Arabic Drama.*

----------, *Now the King is Dead* (1971). G.E.B.O.: Cairo.

----------, *The Princess Waits* (1969). G.E.B.O.: Cairo

----------, *Leila and the Madman* (1972) Ministry of Culture Press, 1998

Al-Salamah, Sikkat, *The Road of Safety* (1965). G.E.B.O.: Cairo.

Al-Salamuni, Abul'Ela, *Revenge: Quest of Pain* (1983). Ministry of Culture Press, 1998.

Salem, Ali, *The Buffet* (1968 one-act). G.E.B.O.: Cairo

----------, *The Comedy of Oedipus* (1970) in *Modern Arabic Drama*.

----------, *The Dogs Reached the Airport*. G.E.B.O.: Cairo, 1997.

----------, *The Wheat Well* (1968) in *Egyptian One-Act Plays*.

Salmawy, Mohammed, *Come Back Tomorrow* , *Next in Line* (both 1983) and *I Shall Tell You All* in *Come Back Tomorrow and Other Plays*. Alef: Cairo,1984.

----------, *Two Down the Drain*. G.E.B.O. Cairo, 1993.

Sarhan, Samir, *The Lady on the Throne*. G.E.B.O.: Cairo, 1972.

Selim, Abdel-Moneim, *Marital Bliss* in *Egyptian One-Act Plays*.

Wahbah, Sa'ad El-Din, *Mosquito Bridge* (1964).G.E.B.O.:Cairo,1987.

----------, *The Road of Safety* (1965). G.E.B.O.: Cairo, 1979)

Note: Those interested in obtaining translations listed above in MS may contact the editor of this volume .

The Martin E. Segal Theatre Center is a non-profit center for theatre, dance, and film affiliated with CUNY's Ph.D Program in Theatre. The Center's mission is to bridge the gap between academia and the professional performing arts communities both within the United States and internationally. By providing an open environment for the development of educational, community-driven, and professional projects in the performing arts, The Segal Center is a home to theatre scholars, students, playwrights, actors, dancers, directors, dramaturgs, and performing arts managers from the local and international theatre communities. Programs include staged readings to further the development of new and classic plays, festivals celebrating New York performance (PRELUDE) and international plays (PEN World Voices: International Play Festival), screenings of performance works on film (Segal Film Festival on Theatre and Performance), artists in conversation, academic lecture series, televized seminars, symposia, and arts in education programs. In addition, the Center maintains its long-standing visiting-scholars-from-abroad program, publishes a series of highly regarded academic journals, as well as single volumes of importance (including plays in translation), all written and edited by renowned scholars.

www.theSegalCenter.org

The PhD Program in Theatre, The Graduate Center, CUNY, is one of the leading doctoral theatre programs in the United States and is The Segal Center's departmental affiliate at The Graduate Center. The Faculty includes distinguished professors, holders of endowed chairs, and internationally recognized scholars. The program trains future scholars and teachers in all the disciplines of theatre research. Faculty members edit MESTC publications, working closely with the doctoral students in theatre who perform a variety of editorial functions and learn the skills involved in the creation of books and journals.

www.gc.cuny.edu/theatre

The Graduate Center, CUNY, of which the Martin E. Segal Theatre Center is an integral part, is the doctorate-granting institution of the City University of New York (CUNY). An internationally recognized center for advanced studies and a national model for public doctoral education, the school offers more than thirty doctoral programs, as well as a number of master's programs. Many of its faculty members are among the world's leading scholars in their respective fields, and its alumni hold major positions in industry and government, as well as in academia. The Graduate Center is also home to twenty-eight interdisciplinary research centers and institutes focused on areas of compelling social, civic, cultural, and scientific concerns. Located in a landmark Fifth Avenue building, The Graduate Center has become a vital part of New York City's intellectual and cultural life with its extensive array of public lectures, exhibitions, concerts, and theatrical events.

www.gc.cuny.edu

IN MEMORIAM: Martin E. Segal (1916–2012), MESTC Founder
Daniel Gerould (1928–2012), MESTC Director of Publications

The Segal Publication Wing includes three open-access digital journals and over twenty-five individual volumes of international plays and theatre resources. The journals are all available for FREE online to a global readership.

Journals

After three decades, the final print editions of *The Journal of American Drama and Theatre (JADT)*, *Slavic and East European Performance (SEEP)*, and *Western European Stages (WES)* were printed in 2013/2014.

The Journal of American Drama and Theatre (JADT) publishes thoughtful and innovative work by leading scholars on theatre, drama, and performance in the U.S.—past and present. Provocative articles provide valuable insight and information on the heritage of American theatre, as well as its continuing contribution to world literature and the performing arts.   www.jadtjournal.org

European Stages (ES) combines the activities of *Western European Stages* and *Slavic and East European Performance* to reflect the contemporary realities of a more integrated continent. Each issue contains a wealth of information about European festivals and productions, including reviews, interviews, and reports.   www.europeanstages.org

Arab Stages (AS) is a new addition to The Segal Center portfolio of digital theatre journals, focusing on contemporary Arab theatre from around the world. It is devoted to broadening international awareness and understanding of the theatre and performance cultures of the Arab-Islamic world and of its diaspora.   www.arabstages.org

Books

Books include *Four Melodramas by Pixérécourt* (edited by Daniel Gerould and Marvin Carlson—both distinguished Professors of Theatre at the CUNY Graduate Center), *Contemporary Theatre in Egypt*, *The Heirs of Molière* (edited and translated by Marvin Carlson), *Seven Plays by Stanisław Ignacy Witkiewicz* (edited and translated by Daniel Gerould), *The Arab Oedipus: Four Plays* (edited by Marvin Carlson), *Theatre Research Resources in New York City* (edited by Jessica Brater, Senior Editor Marvin Carlson), *Comedy: A Bibliography of Critical Studies in English on the Theory and Practice of Comedy in Drama, Theatre, and Performance* (edited by Meghan Duffy, Senior Editor Daniel Gerould), *BAiT-Buenos Aires in Translation: Four Plays* (edited and translated by Jean Graham-Jones), *roMANIA AFTER 2000: Five New Romanian Plays* (edited by Saviana Stanescu and Daniel Gerould), *Four Plays from North Africa* (edited by Marvin Carlson), *Barcelona Plays: A Collection of New Plays by Catalan Playwrights* (edited and translated by Marion Peter Holt and Sharon G. Feldman), *Josep M. Benet i Jornet: Two Plays* (edited and translated by Marion Peter Holt), *Czech Plays: Seven New Works* (edited by Marcy Arlin, Gwynn MacDonald and Daniel Gerould), *Playwrights before the Fall* (edited by Daniel Gerould), *Timbre 4* (edited and translated by Jean Graham-Jones), *Jan Fabre: The Servant of Beauty and I Am a Mistake* (edited and foreword by Frank Hentschker), *Quick Change: 28 Theatre Essays and 4 Plays in Translation* (by Daniel Gerould), *Shakespeare Made French: Four Plays by Jean-François Ducis* (edited and translated by Marvin Carlson), *New Plays from Spain: Eight Works by Seven Playwrights* (edited by Frank Hentschker), *Four Plays From Syria: Sa'dallah Wannous* (edited by Marvin Carlson and Safi Mahfouz), *Four Millennial Plays From Belgium* (edited and translated by David Willinger), *Szertelen Színdarabok New Yorkból/Riff Raff Plays from New York - ARC (Advanced Readers Copy)* (edited by Attila Szabó and Frank Hentschker, translated into Hungarian by Attila Szabó & Noémi Keckés), *The Trilogy of Future Memory: Jalila Baccar & Fadhel Jaïbi* (edited by Marvin Carlson), *Decadent Histories: Four Plays by Amelia Hertz* (translated and edited by Jadwiga Kosicka), and *Four Arab Hamlet Plays* (edited by Marvin Carlson & Margaret Litvin with Joy Arab).

For more information, please visit www.theSegalCenter.org/publications